Godless Armageddon

Godless Armageddon

Scott Coon

HYPATIA
PRESS

Published by Hypatia Press in the United Kingdom in 2024

ISBN: 978-1-83919-671-3

www.hypatiapress.org

I dedicate this book to the Writers of Sherman Oaks, especially Rebekah 'K' Boning (who said, "You should write that."), Janet Wertman, Gerry Gainford, Alex Caine, LS Quigley, Rebecca Stanley, Elain Licas, Sam Scolari, Chelsea Poole, Kit Replogle, Shawn V. Wilson…and to my girlfriend Mary Leta Morgan for all her support.

Chapter 1
I Died

This is not a bible. If someone presents this book to you as a religious text, they are feeding you a line. I'm dead and I'm writing this through a living surrogate, but I am not a god, nor is anyone else in the afterlife. If anyone from here contacts you, claiming to be some kind of a divine being, don't fall for it. They're lying. They're selfish. And they're indulging themselves in a way that endangers your soul and the soul of every person, living and dead, throughout human history. That is why I am telling this story; that is why I am putting this poor guy through the trauma of hearing my disembodied voice in his head; my purpose is to prevent that. So, for the sake of all human souls and this man's sanity, let me begin.

As one might expect from someone in the afterlife, the story I have to tell starts on the day I died, when I was still Staff Sergeant Thomas Jefferson Stoneshield VII...

***

"There're no atheists in foxholes," came the cliché from the soldier behind Staff Sergeant Thomas "Thom" Jefferson Stoneshield VII.

1

"Well, there's one on this boat!" Thom yelled back at Sergeant Peterson, while the engines gurgled and roared.

"Two!" yelled Corporal Johnston from in front of Thom.

"Two and a half…I guess," Corporal David Lowenstein said. Looking over his shoulder at Johnston and Thom, he added, "Agnostic."

Thom was wedged in the middle of his squad of U.S. Army Rangers in the landing craft with Peterson crammed right up behind him. Peterson's little buddy, Corporal Corbin, was right there with him. It was hard enough to focus while bouncing from whitecap to whitecap, his stomach flipping like flapjacks. Hearing one of Peterson's sermons wouldn't help. Thom needed to focus on the mission and getting his men through it alive.

They were headed for Pointe du Hoc to take out the guns overlooking the beaches of Normandy. At least, they were supposed to be. Thom couldn't see the other boats, or the cliffs, only grey mist and choppy water. The mission hadn't even started yet, and it was already belly up. And Peterson couldn't shut up.

"It's not too late," Peterson bellowed in Thom's ear. "Find trust in the Lord and he will see you through."

Johnston said, "You're barking up the wrong heathen. He's got *atheist* on his dog tags."

"They let you do that?" Corbin asked.

"Not possible," Peterson said. "They wouldn't."

"No really," Johnston said. "He kept sending them back until they did it. Hey, Stoneshield, show 'em your tags."

Thom fished his tags out from under his layers of clothes and gear, then tossed them over his shoulder. Peterson tugged them tight around Thom's neck, the thin chain threatening to break with each bounce of the boat. If Thom lost them and he died, his body could go unidentified. Not that Thom had anyone to collect his remains. He didn't even have anyone to visit for his last leave before shipping out. He ended up wandering the streets of New York.

His dad died back in the first great war. His mother had died before he enlisted. Even his best friend, Gregory, had died somewhere in Italy. His closest relative would be one of his second cousins, but he didn't really know any of them. There was Great Uncle Marv, his grandfather's brother, but Thom hadn't seen him in so long that he was pretty sure Great Uncle Marv was gone too. If Thom kicked the bucket, here, today, it wouldn't matter much to anyone. No one would want his remains.

"Blasphemy," Peterson said, still holding the chain.

"How could you do that to your soul?" Corbin said.

Thom pulled his dog tags free. "Actually, it was all my soul's idea."

He tucked them away and returned to looking for the other boats, or even the cliffs of Pointe du Hoc. The men on the beaches needed them to complete this mission, even if their boat had to do it alone.

"Sent your tags back what—two, three times before they put atheist on 'em?" Johnston asked. "Ain't that right, Stoneshield? Me, all I got was 'no preference.' Hey, Lowenstein, what'd you get?"

"Jew." David Lowenstein fired the word like a bullet. "And I'm gonna shove it in the face of every Nazi Kraut from here to Berlin."

Thom got up on his toes, trying to see out ahead of them, past the bow of their landing craft, known as a DUKW, which they pronounced *duck*. But he couldn't see anything except for dark sky and choppy water. The extension ladder from the London Fire Brigade wasn't helping. It'd been slapped on their boat at the last minute. They already had grappling hooks and pipe ladders. The extension ladder was redundant, heavy, and reduced stability. They'd be lucky to make it ashore without capsizing.

And where the hell were the other boats?

"Don't worry, Sergeant Stoneshield," Peterson said. "I'll pray for your soul."

Johnston shoved his way past Thom to shake a fist in Peterson's face. "Try praying for my soul and I'll punch you in the mouth, you poof."

Thom turned to snarl at Johnston and his word for queer. Maybe it was the sound, maybe it was the way kids threw it at each other when he was growing up, he didn't know, but Thom had always hated that word, *poof.* Right now, it made him want to punch Johnston in the mouth.

Peterson blessed Johnston. Johnston cocked his fist. Before he could throw it, Thom shoved Johnston back a step. "Knock it off! We don't need you two mixing it up!"

From the back of the boat, Sergeant First Class Williamson roared, "What's the trouble up there?" When no one answered him, he yelled, "Save it for the Krauts!"

A long silence followed, underscored by the gurgling and growling of the engines lifting into the air, then flopping back into the brine with a slap and a sputter. Light seeped into the sky, thinning the grey mist, but not enough to see anything.

Thom asked, "Anybody got eyes on the other boats?"

Everyone looked but no one saw anything.

"We won't try to take the cliffs alone, right?" Corbin asked, his words fast and choppy like the whitecaps hitting their hull. "I mean, we'd fall in with the others on the beach, right?"

"With this weather," David Lowenstein said, "we'll be pulled back. It ain't today."

"Yeah," Corbin said, his voice easing. "It would take a miracle to land today."

"Ask and the Lord shall provide," Peterson said.

Johnston shook his head. "Weather ain't no miracle."

"All of life is a Miracle," Peterson said.

Johnston snorted. "Yeah, *this* is a miracle, a regular European vacation."

"I always wanted to see Europe." Corbin forced a chuckle.

"Didn't your father die here, Stoneshield?" Johnston said.

"Flanders Fields."

Thom's words lingered long after they'd been devoured by the engines and waves. Thom could feel his comrades comparing their current mission to that suicidal disaster from the first great war, where soldiers were ordered to senselessly charge into mud and machine gun fire. Glancing around, he found them all staring down at the seawater and motor oil sloshing over their boots.

"I lived here," David said, ending the moment, "I was German…until I was nine. My parents are still here…maybe. I'm planning to go looking for them…after…if I can."

"What're you gonna desert and go searching all over Europe?" Johnston asked.

"If I have to."

"After all the bombs we dropped on the Krauts," Johnston said, "you really think you'll find your parents?"

David clenched his jaw. "I don't know, but I'll try, right after we kill every Nazi from here to Berlin."

Thom knew the odds were against David. Even if the worst rumors weren't true, even if what happened in Warsaw wasn't what the Nazis were doing to all the Jews, this was still war—a world war. America's B-17s pounded the German cities every night while Britain's Lancasters pounded them every day.

But at least David had a chance of finding his parents alive. All Thom had was his dad's folded flag, his mom's Saint Christopher medal, and a letter from Gregory's sister telling Thom that his best friend was dead. With no one to ship it home to, the folded flag had to stay back at Thom's last duty station in England. But he wore the medal and kept the letter tucked close to his heart. It was all he had left of Gregory.

They'd met in basic training and fought together across Africa. They became inseparable, even taking leave together. When the war turned to Europe, the army sent Thom to England and Gregory to Sicily. The last thing Gregory said to Thom was, "I'll see you in Berlin." It didn't matter that Gregory wasn't able to keep that promise. Thom probably wouldn't make it either. He didn't expect most of the men on this boat to live through the day. Even if they did, the odds of any of them surviving to see Berlin were slim.

But Thom's life didn't matter as much as his name. The name Thomas Jefferson Stoneshield VII was his birthright and his responsibility, one that he'd failed. Though twenty-seven, he had no kids, not even a wife. He hadn't gotten around to it. Now there'd never be a Thomas Jefferson Stoneshield VIII, and it was all his fault.

Thom pushed the thoughts from his head and went back to looking for the other boats. As the rising sun thinned the fog, he saw a landing craft bobbing off to the right. He felt a little better but not much. They started with twelve boats, but he could only find one other. And they had to be getting close to shore. Thom looked off toward the back of their boat, hoping to spot at least one more landing craft.

Then Williamson bellowed, "Take a gander, gentlemen."

Thom turned forward. What he saw tossed his stomach more than the floundering sea. The tall, natural walls of Pointe du Hoc towered over the beach—a beach that was nothing more than a narrow band of sand with no cover. It seemed impossible, but Thom kept staring at the cliffs, planning and calculating. They had to reach the top and destroy those guns.

"I'm not ready to die," Corbin mumbled.

"Whatever happens today," Peterson said, "trust in the Lord and He will see you through."

From under his coat, Corbin fished out his cross necklace, kissed it, and began chanting The Lord's Prayer. Peterson joined him. Thom almost wished he believed in that stuff. He remembered going to church when he was little. But when his single mom couldn't afford the time or the collection plate, it stopped.

As the fog continued to thin, more boats appeared around them, including the other DUKW. Thom felt better but not much. Studying the cliffs, thinking about their training, he wondered if the grappling hooks and pipe ladders would reach. It looked like the boat's extension ladder would be useless, but Thom hoped he was wrong.

At the top of the cliffs, there was a flash. Then a mortar screamed out of the sky and plunked into the English Channel, unexploded. Another quickly followed. Then another and another. While the rest of his team crouched below the metal walls of the craft, Thom remained standing, studying the cliffs, surveying the locations of the mortar emplacements, planning his team's assault.

More shells fell, each splashing into the brine until one landed with a boom. Looking left, Thom saw the other DUKW billowing smoke as it sank beneath the swells.

Bullets joined the mortars, plinking off the boat's armor while shells continued plunking into the sea. Still, Thom stood, studying their target, planning their way up the cliff, and looking for the big gun emplacements. Why weren't they firing?

A fist grabbed his coat. "What're you doin'?" Johnston yelled, trying to pull Thom down. "Keep your fucking head d—"

A bullet ripped the last word from Johnston's throat. Blood splattered Thom's gear and clothes. As Johnston sank to his knees, choking, Thom called for the medic.

By the time their corpsman shoved his way forward, Johnston was gone. Having done nothing, the medic returned to the back. Johnston's blood mixed with the seawater and motor oil. It sloshed back and forth over everyone's boots, while Thom stood there staring down at Johnston's blank eyes.

"Get your fucking head down!" Williamson barked from the back.

Thom got his fucking head down.

**

The gurgling engines were overshadowed by the rising rhythm of the plinks and plunks. Above it all, Williamson shouted instructions and encouragement in equal measure.

"The second we land, I want the ladders up and the grappling hooks fired. Use the boats for cover or stay tight to the cliff. Once we reach the top, fire the flares to call in reinforcements. We will get up there and we will take out those guns. That is our mission. We cannot and will not fail. Remember your training, work together, and we'll all get through this."

That last part was a lie, and the proof lay beneath Thom as he squatted in the boat. Yet another man had left Thom covered in blood. The first time had been in Casablanca. The second time, Thom no longer remembered.

David Lowenstein gripped Thom's shoulder. Eyes cold, he said, "It's not your fault."

He was wrong. But Thom replied with a firm nod and nothing more.

Heavy shells ripped across the sky and crashed upon the clifftops. The battleships had begun their barrage. The German mortars and gunfire tapered off, but the bombardment wasn't entirely helpful. Shells fell short, ripping up the beach, what little there was, turning the smooth slope into craters and dunes. With gunfire coming straight down, the dunes would be obstacles but not cover.

Under the screech and thunder of artillery, Corbin and Peterson chanted The Lord's Prayer with rising fervor. "Our Father who art in heaven, Hallowed be Thy name. Thy kingdom come. Thy will be done on earth as it is in Heaven."

As they neared the beach, the battleships walked their bombardment back, giving them room to land. The renewed gunfire rattled the hull. The driver pushed the throttle to full. The groaning engines echoed off the rockface back at them.

Williamson yelled, "Brace yourselves!"

They slammed ashore, stopping hard on the lip of a shell crater. Everyone lurched forward, nearly knocking Thom onto Johnston's body.

"Over the sides!" Williamson ordered.

Everyone jumped out and ran for the cliff, but Thom and Williamson stayed to grab gear. With one glance, Thom knew the London Fire Brigade extension ladder wouldn't reach anything. So, he went for a pipe ladder hanging off the side of the boat instead. Williamson helped him wrestle it off. As two more boats landed, the ladder came free. Thom dragged it to the cliff, while Williamson took cover under the DUKW's bow, returning fire at the cliff above.

He yelled, "Grappling hooks! Now!"

Four men stepped out and launched their rocket-propelled hooks. With wet ropes weighing them down, they all fell short.

"Get the ladders!"

While Williamson and others gave covering fire, six Rangers ran for more ladders.

Staying flat to the cliff, David joined Thom and shoved his ladder up the rockface. As soon as they had it up, someone above pushed it away from the cliff. Thom and David fought to keep it against the rock. Peterson and Corbin joined them, but they still couldn't seat it.

The resistance suddenly stopped. A body thudded onto the sand beside them. It wore a Nazi uniform and had no face. Still under the boat, Williamson nodded, confirming his kill. Then machinegun fire raked his chest, killing Williamson. The shock of watching it staggered Thom. He quickly shook it off and continued the mission.

Over the gunfire and explosions, David yelled, "I'm going!"

Thom nodded and held the ladder firm against the cliff. Peterson held it from the other side. David went up. More bullets came down. One ripped through Thom's jacket, grazing his arm. He stayed at the ladder.

Peterson waved for Corbin to go next. Corbin only got five rungs under him before Thom saw the grenade. It flipped end over end mere inches from his face. He barely had time to recognize what it was before it hit Peterson's boot and exploded.

***

For a moment, Thom thought the grenade had thrown him into the air. But he wasn't falling back down. Instead, he hovered. A few feet below him, he saw Peterson, his missing leg gushing blood into the sand. Beside Peterson lay Corbin, a medic hunched over his unconscious body, trying to keep him alive. Then Thom saw himself.

Though his face had been shredded by shrapnel, he recognized his own body. He was dead. At least, it seemed that way. Hovering there, Thom still felt alive. He even looked like himself, gear and all hanging in midair. Maybe he wasn't dead; maybe he was unconscious, imagining this.

Looking back at his own faceless body, Thom realized that it was getting farther away. He was drifting up, floating past David Lowenstein who was still climbing the ladder. Thom passed the clifftop and kept going into the sky.

David reached the crest and threw himself over. He had only a shallow depression for cover against the heavy incoming fire, but he got off his flare. From the sky, Thom looked out into the Channel. He saw no help coming. David was signaling to no one.

As Thom rose ever higher, David, the cliff, and the Earth itself faded into blackness, as if they ceased to exist. A gold fog enveloped Thom. There was no ground, no sky, no other people. There was only Thom and his gear rising through the shimmering mist. All was silent, until urgent words came from above.

"I gotta get back to my men. They need me."

Thom looked up to see his platoon sergeant plummeting through the glowing gold. "Williamson! What's happening?"

As he fell past, Williamson repeated, "I gotta get back to my men. They need me."

Williamson's words faded behind a rising chant. It was Peterson and Corbin, still together, still reciting the Lord's Prayer. They rose fast, overtaking Thom. Before his eyes, their bodies and gear melted into man-sized clouds. Peterson's fog was red and Corbin's green. Unlike the glittering gold fog that surrounded them, their clouds were dim and muddy. Even without bodies, they continued their chant.

More men shot up through the haze, all in their uniforms, some Allied, some Nazi, all melting into murky clouds of red, blue, or green. Thom looked at his hands. He grabbed at his gear. It remained solid. Why? He was dead. He had to be. He couldn't be anything else. Why wasn't he melting like all the others?

Out of the fog came the sound of church bells. But they lacked that moment when the clapper hit the side, jolting the bells into quivers, but they quivered, nonetheless. The percussion-less ring undulated through a slow, swinging rhythm of vibrating bronze. The farther Thom rose, the louder they got. The clap-less clangs rolled through his body, crushing the air from his lungs. Vainly gasping, he watched his equipment dissolve into haze, then his clothes, and finally himself. But he still felt like a person with a body, like when soldiers lose limbs but still feel them. Only it wasn't Thom's arm or leg. It was all of him.

Thom tried to look at his hands but saw two mounds of dark blue haze instead. Looking up toward the sound, Thom's gaze fell

13

upon a massive black octopus like something off the cover of a dime store adventure novel. Its perfectly round head had to be as tall as four New York City skyscrapers, stacked. At its base, eight long tentacles surrounded a dark round mouth.

The black arms swung through the golden fog, barely missing Thom but sweeping up many other cloud-people. As it passed, Thom realized the monster was made of oily black smoke, as thick as a tire fire. When the arms curled in with the captured souls, the mouth opened into a swirling vortex, like Charybdis of ancient Greece, sucking the souls into its dark whirlpool.

Watching it, Thom's brain went numb. He'd stared into the barrels of enemy machine guns and stood before tanks about to fire, but nothing chilled him like the impossible sight floating above him.

Over the surreal bells, Thom heard Peterson chanting with rising fervor. "The Lord is my shepherd, I shall not want!" Peterson's cloud glowed bright red as it sped toward the giant smoke octopus.

"I'm not sure that's God," Corbin's murky green cloud called to him.

Thom pulled his head together and yelled, "I don't know what that is, but it's not your god. It's not any god."

"Lean not on your own understanding. Submit to Him, and He will make your paths straight," Peterson said, his cloud glowing brighter and brighter. Reaching the cusp of the mouth, his bright cloud abruptly darkened. He turned and sent ripples rolling down his body, as if trying to swim away from it. He started moving toward escape, but a tentacle returned with another harvest, the whirlpool-mouth opened wide, and Peterson was pulled in with the others.

Corbin hung there adrift, silently staring at it, his mist growing darker and thinner, as if he might cease to exist at all.

Thom needed to get Corbin out of there before they both ended up like Peterson. But how? Could they even move? Peterson did, with that rippling thing. Thom tried swimming, pumping his arms and legs like he still had them. Somehow, it worked. In his head, he was swimming like a person. But in reality, he was rippling waves down his blue cloud body to move it through the golden fog.

"Swim!" he cried up to Corbin over the relentless bells. "You can escape! Imagine yourself swimming!"

"Stoneshield? Is that you?"

Loaded with more souls, another smoke tentacle swung its tip back in towards the mouth, back towards Corbin.

Thom yelled, "Swim, Corbin! Hurry!"

Finally, Corbin began rippling, propelling himself upward and away from the ravenous arms. The dark limbs swung past, collecting more souls, but missing Corbin. He continued his frantic climb, getting himself beyond the monster's reach. Thom thought Corbin was safe, until a new sound rolled from the golden fog. It was the drone of church hymns, the words vague, the melody familiar but unclear. The hymns mixed with the bells to create a discordant cascade of surreal noise.

From the fog and hymns, more giant tentacles emerged. One captured Corbin and many others. It returned its harvest to a second giant octopus of black smoke. Its massive round head was bigger than the first monster's by at least a skyscraper. Corbin and the others were lost. But Thom remained, now floating between the two enormous beasts. He swam faster, hoping against hope to rise above them before one of the many tentacles got him.

A new glowing soul rose from below, a gold cloud much denser and brighter than the fog around it. The soul sped up toward Thom and into the maelstrom of swinging arms. Both monsters forsook their harvesting to grab the glowing soul. They each latched onto it with all eight arms. As they fought to rip the soul from the other's grasp, the tiny cloud glowed brighter and brighter. More clouds rose from below, but the giants ignored them.

Thom heard the glowing soul screaming in German. It was only a boy, and he was in pain. The giants continued to pull. Thom wanted to go help the boy, but how?

Squeezed by the smoke arms, the boy's soul grew brighter, his screams louder, until in a silent flash, he exploded.

A sphere of green electricity swelled out from the epicenter, hurtling toward Thom. He swam up, but it was inescapable. The spreading lightning overtook him. Thom felt it rip through his body, even though he didn't have one. He thought he'd explode like that boy. But then he found himself back in a human body, back on Earth.

Thom was suddenly lying on his belly, looking over a cliff at the sea far below. The gold fog, cloud people, and giant smoke monsters were all gone. The Earth had returned, and Thom had a body with real arms and legs.

Someone fired up at him from the narrow beach. Thom fired back, missing, then retreated from the edge. It was then that Thom realized he was surrounded by Nazis, and that he was a Nazi too. Thom was the German boy, but Thom was also still Thom, existing as two people at one time.

His commander grabbed German-boy-Thom by the coat and yelled in German, "Get back to the edge! Fire! Fire!"

Thom understood and obeyed. He crawled back to the edge and spotted a target. The part of Thom that was the German boy didn't recognize the American taking cover under the boat. But the part of Thom that was still Thom did recognize him. It was his platoon sergeant, Williamson. Thom wanted to stop the boy from firing, but he had no power here. He was only along for the ride.

He took aim. All he had to do was pull the trigger. It was why he was there—to pull the trigger. But the German boy's father had been a devout Lutheran and a pacifist. The boy was too. He couldn't pull the trigger. He wouldn't. He wasn't going to become a killer for his fatherland. He emptied his clip into open sand, hitting no one.

On the beach, Williamson aimed at the boy and fired. Again, Thom found himself floating up. Below, he saw his body—the German boy's body—slip over the edge, falling to the beach below, his face destroyed by Williamson's bullet. Thom recognized this moment. He'd seen this boy's body hit the beach; it was just before Williamson died, and before Thom died.

Then the memory ended.

When Thom came out of the memory, he found himself still drifting up through the gold fog. Gradually, Thom felt like Thom again, not Thom and a young German boy at the same time. Thom looked at his hands again. They were back to being nebulous mounds of swirling blue gas—a dark, mournful blue.

Gazing down, he saw the two black octopus-monsters now far, far below. The larger one was harvesting alone while the smaller retreated, cutting a dark wake through the glimmering fog as it left. It had closed its mouth and drawn its long tentacles into its body, leaving it just a giant ball of black smoke. To move, it rippled its body, swimming like Thom had. Was that thing a soul? Thom could only guess.

He looked around for other souls or signs of heaven or hell or Valhalla or something. He saw only the gold fog.

"I'm a soul," he told himself, as he grew a darker blue. "I'm dead. I'm a soul. And I've failed everyone."

Chapter 2
Judgment

Other than up, Thom didn't know where he was going. Gazing down at the grim harvest, he couldn't imagine that there'd be gates of pearl or lakes of fire somewhere above. But he could imagine meeting his father and his grandfather—perhaps his whole male line back to the Battle of Dunbar, when the name Stoneshield was first bestowed upon them. He imagined them standing in judgment of Thomas Jefferson Stoneshield VII, the Stoneshield who ended their legacy.

Thom deserved their judgment. He'd failed them all. Especially his father, a war hero who died young but left Thom behind to continue the family name. Thom had died childless at twenty-seven. He selfishly spent his time hunting, fishing, acting like a kid when he was supposed to be a man, getting married, having a family.

As Thom drifted toward the unknown, he thought he could hear his father's voice. The words were faint and far off, muffled behind the nebulous hymns coming from the giant smoke octopus below. Focusing harder, Thom was almost certain that his father said, "I'm sorry, Son. I shouldn't have done that to you."

"Done what?" Thom called back. "You were dead. What could you have done?"

But the apology only repeated, his father's words growing more faint with each moment. Thom tried to swim down, but his arms and legs were gone, both from his body and his mind. His momentum continued upward, while he gazed down at the lone monster lashing its limbs through the rising clusters of souls. Soon, Thom couldn't hear his father at all.

The gold fog around Thom thinned. He gazed up and saw a shimmering plain, as if he were rising out of deep water, toward the surface of a sunlit lake. Thom's cloud-body broke the surface and stopped. His once globular form spread into a puddle of dark blue haze upon a sea of dense gold fog.

"I failed them," Thom admitted, still awaiting some kind of condemnation. "Family and country, I failed them all."

But his confession went unjudged. From his puddle, Thom gazed up, expecting to see a court room, a church, a bearded man, or anyone to preside over him. Instead, he saw stars…but something was wrong with them. There were far fewer than he was used to seeing, and none were white. Many twinkled with gold, but others had dark shades of red, green, and blue.

As he stared, something floated across his view about a mile above him, a storm cloud swirling with muted hues of red. Unlike normal clouds adrift on the wind, this one seemed to move with intention. He saw another just like it, only green, and then another that was pink. Above these smaller nebulous clouds passed a much larger storm with blue arms swirling like a pinwheel around a hazy, dark blue orb. And above that storm, another even larger storm that had arms of gold pivoting around an orb of solid silver.

As he gazed upon the storms, he heard someone calling out, someone who had pooled upon the surface near him.

"Keep your fucking head down!" they yelled. "Do you want to get it blown off?"

Like a worm, Thom inched his fog-self across the golden surface. Around him, he saw other puddles, as well as small, low-lying clouds. Thom guessed them to be souls, like himself.

"Keep your head down!" came the call again.

Thom slunk toward the sound, until he found a blue puddle of mist so dark it was nearly black.

"Keep your head down!" it yelled. "…shot off. Your head…shot off. Stoneshield?"

"Johnston?" Thom asked.

"Stoneshield? Ya got your head shot off. Got mine shot off too, didn't ya?"

"I did," Thom confessed, as his cloud body gathered into a lump. "I got you killed. I'm so sorry."

"Ha," Johnston said, "an illusion apologizing. I'm dead but my brain don't know it yet. And what's it give me for my last moments? You, the knuckle head that got me killed. *Great.*"

"I'm not an illusion," Thom told him. "I don't know where we are, but it's not your head."

The puddle merely chuckled, the sound growing fainter as the fog thinned.

"Johnston, stay with me," Thom begged.

Johnston continued to fade. Thom reached out with what he still expected to be arms. What extended before him appeared to be a pair of smoke tentacles, like from those giants. With them, Thom reached under the thinning puddle that was Johnston to pick him up. When Thom touched him, he fell into another memory.

Thom was Thom, but he was also Johnston crouching in the DUKW. He watched the seawater slosh over his boot, soaking his socks. It would almost be worth it to kick the bucket just to not have wet socks. Looking up, Thom—who was Johnston—saw that knucklehead, Stoneshield, sticking his head up like they were on a Sunday drive.

"Keep your fucking head down!" Johnston yelled. He reached for the front of Stoneshield's jacket. "Do you want to get it blown off?"

He pulled down on Stoneshield's uniform but found his hand empty. He realized his boots were no longer in the boat. His socks were still wet, but he'd lifted out of the water and was floating up. Looking down, he saw someone lying dead at Stoneshield's feet. When he realized it was his own body, Johnston said, "That knucklehead got me killed."

The memory faded. Thom became only Thom again, a lump of blue mist on a sea of gold fog. He found his smoke tentacles hanging empty in front of him. The haze that had been Johnston was gone. Guilt caved in on him. He did get Johnston killed. Johnston was his soldier, and Thom's actions got him killed. And now even his soul had vanished.

Looking around, Thom found another dark blue puddle just in time to watch it fade from existence. It wasn't Johnston, Thom could feel it. But Johnston was gone, he could feel that too. Thom had gotten Johnston killed once. But had to watch him die twice. He melted back into a murky puddle.

***

"Yup, another one gone," said a voice from somewhere above.

"That soul shall soon fade as well," said another, referring to Thom. "This new Great War does not bode well for their planet."

"I think they're calling it the Second World War now," said the first voice, which Thom somehow knew to be Snake. It had other names but preferred Snake. "I guess they're planning to keep count of their World Wars," Snake added.

"What made us think that other worlds would fare any better than either of ours?" said the other voice, which belonged to someone who preferred the name Prometheus above his others, though Thom didn't know how he knew that. "It seems an inevitability," Prometheus continued. "Every species of technological sentience appears bent on self-destruction. We are all snakes eating our tails."

Snake said, "Oh, lighten up. They ain't dead yet. Like this guy. He ain't dead yet. Are you, Thom? You're not dead."

Unable to see the owners of the voices from his flat vantage point, Thom asked, "Who are you?"

"I told you, I'm Snake."

"No, you didn't," Thom said, not sure he was right.

"Well, I did, and I didn't," Snake said.

Prometheus said, "He still thinks he's using his living senses. That means he will soon fade, as I warned."

"He could sink, too, you know. But you're not gonna fade or sink, are you, Thom? You're gonna stay with us."

Fading. Sinking. Thom had seen Williamson falling back down. He'd been eager to get back to Earth. And Thom had seen that other soul fade away, just like Johnston must've faded. Thom didn't want to fade or sink. He wanted to live, whatever living meant now.

Thom pulled himself together and lifted a part of himself out of his puddle. Looking across the flat golden surface, he again saw other dark puddles of haze, most of them fading. But one nearby puddle rose from the surface, ascending toward the three layers of colorful clouds above. The soul passed through the lower layer of pillowy clouds, to the upper layer where it vanished into the great pinwheel of dark blue clouds circling an orb of even darker blue.

Prometheus said, "Another soul has joined the choir of Nietzsche."

Thom turned toward the voice and found two solid silver orbs floating a few feet away from him, each appeared as wide as a man was tall. The orb on the right said, "Hey, Thom's going to make it. I told you so." Thom somehow knew this orb to be Snake.

"My condolences regarding your friend, Johnston," Prometheus said.

"But good effort trying to save him," Snake said. "It was pointless but a good effort."

"What happened to him?" Thom asked.

"He died, all-the-way died," Snake said.

"He failed to exist," Prometheus explained. "He didn't have the willpower to hold his life energy together, so he faded away. His life energy has been dispersed. The willpower that made that energy Johnston is no more. There is no Johnston."

Thom shivered, or at least he felt like he was shivering. He couldn't be sure about it or anything, really, other than he didn't want to all-the-way die.

"But that won't happen to you," Snake assured Thom. "You'll be a free soul like us."

Thom muttered, "A what soul?"

"A free soul...not part of a choir or consumed by a soul well," Prometheus told him.

"Soul well?"

"Yes," Prometheus said. "Your planet has two, Alpha and Unum. They're the dark harvesters you saw below, the ones you believed to be octopi."

"And you got about a hundred choirs right now." Snake's orb grew a stubby, pudgy nub that pointed toward the clouds above.

"You need not fear the choirs," Prometheus said. "A choir is not like a well. The individuals within choirs retain their own willpower."

Snake said, "But in soul wells, there's one selfish person in the middle, sucking up everyone else's willpower...the greedy jerk. Keeps them all locked in nightmares too. But choirs are nice, like the choir of Buddha. That's it, there." Snake pointed toward the largest of the spiraling pinwheels, the one with arms of gold orbiting a silver sphere.

As Thom focused on it, he heard it speak…or think…or something. "If you fear, if you grieve, we are here for you. We will help you reach nirvana. Join our choir and we will care for you." Around Thom, puddles gathered themselves and floated up. Most joined Buddha. Many others joined Nietzsche. Just a few joined the smaller puffy clouds hovering below them.

Snake told Thom, "If you focus a little more, you'll experience a memory from a choir, get an idea of what it's like in there, see if you wanna join."

Thom focused on the choir called Buddha. He focused until, once again, Thom was Thom and also someone else, a monk this time. The monk sat in the courtyard of a monastery, with curving tiled roofs and dragons and monkeys adorning the walls. He sat alone in the moonlight, holding a small clay jar filled with a silver liquid.

It was supposed to be a magic potion, a shortcut to nirvana. Thom the monk had been seeking nirvana for a long time, spending long hours in meditation, studying texts, trying to grasp that elusive state of being. His efforts lacked focus and he knew it—his mind always wandering, never clear. But this clay jar held the key to becoming one with the Buddha. Found in an ancient alchemical tome, the potion was mostly mercury and arsenic. He drank.

Thom, who was the monk, assumed the lotus position and waited for enlightenment. Instead, his guts burned. Thom fell forward onto his hands and knees. Head pounding, body shaking, Thom gasped for air. The potion, it was not a path to nirvana, only death. But it was already too late, he'd killed himself like a fool.

Before the sun crested the distant Mountains, Thom the monk was dead.

When he reached the surface of the golden ocean, he felt that he deserved to fade from existence. But the Buddha felt otherwise and welcomed Thom into his choir where he could again walk the path toward enlightenment.

***

When it ended, Thom felt like he'd fallen out of the memory and landed with a thud. His body had again spread into a murky puddle upon the glittering gold.

Hovering near him, the orb of Snake said, "Ain't that like your third memory? You should be used to it by now."

"He does not look used to it by now," Prometheus said.

"You okay, kid?"

Still lost between identities, Thom focused his thoughts on the now, willing himself to be himself and only himself. Feeling more stable, Thom's cloud grew. It rose from the surface and hovered a few feet in the air like Prometheus and Snake. Still, he remained a thin dark blue haze, not a solid silver orb, like them. And he was less than half their size.

"Hey, you're getting yourself together," Snake said. "Good for you."

Thom asked, "What's nirvana?"

"In your fiction and philosophy, it is many things," Prometheus explained. "But in our existence, it is to become a fully realized soul, as we are, and as the soul of Buddha is."

Thom said, "You mean that silver ball up there, that's actually Buddha? The oriental god, Buddha? He's real?"

"Yes, he is," Snake said. "But people don't like being called *oriental*...and while we're on the subject, you can get a head start on not using *kraut*. But, yes, that's really Buddha in there. Nice guy. Alive, he was really beefy for someone who sat around a lot. His Earthly depictions are all over the place, though. None look anything like him."

"Our Earthly depictions are quite inaccurate as well," Prometheus said, "always turning us into humans or animals."

"Your depictions? As animals and *humans*?" Thom asked. Everything that had happened to him from the moment he died forward, it all piled into his brain, overwhelming his understanding of everything. Nothing made sense. His mind spun. "You mean you're not people? Or not from Earth? Are you Martians? And how am I hearing you? And seeing you? I'm a cloud! And you're...you're...what the hell are you? What am I? I mean, I know I'm dead. I died. I'm dead but...but...everything. Everything else. What the hell is everything else! What in the holy hell is going on!"

Prometheus hovered closer and said, "You are understandably confused."

"Let me explain," Snake said.

"No," Prometheus said, "don't let him explain. Let me explain. It'll be more effective."

"What does that mean?!" Snake demanded. Prometheus did not reply. After a brief silence, Snake said, "Yeah, let him explain."

Thom asked, "What are you two?"

"We're Martians," Snake said.

"No, we are not from Mars," Prometheus corrected him. "We are from other planets around other stars that are not your Sun. And Snake and I are not from the same star. We did not meet until we each came to your planet, separately."

"Prometheus got here first," Snake said.

"Thor arrived first," Prometheus said. "Though he is gone now."

"If you're not from Mars," Thom said, "then where are you guys from? Venus?"

"No, not Venus," Snake said, "that's still a planet around your star. I thought you humans knew about solar systems?"

"Do you see the lights above?" Prometheus asked. "What you see are not the stars. You can no longer perceive matter, like stars and planets and the living. You can only see the life energy of souls expressed as emotions. Thus, each light in the sky is the emotional radiation from the souls surrounding a planet. Snake and I came from distant lights like those you see now. But the light of the souls around our planets have been extinguished, as yours shall be one day."

Snake said, "There's that Prometheus optimism I love."

"Like your planet, my planet once had two soul wells," Prometheus continued, his solid silver shell dimming as if tarnished. "I stood apart from those massive orbs and tried to help others do the same. I failed and once one soul well had defeated the other,

29

it became our *Armageddon*...a relentless monster that consumes all souls...dead...or living..."

As Prometheus trailed off, Snake said, "Yeah, so, that's the thing we came here to do, to help you...well, not you specifically, like whoever became the technologically sentient species. I got here third, but I still got here before you did. I mean, I got here before you evolved. Prometheus and Thor were already here but, other than them, your afterlife was pretty empty...except for the gold, of course. There'd been so many non-sentient and calm-sentient beings on your planet that your afterlife already had a very healthy animalsphere."

"Animalsphere?" Thom asked.

"All that glowing stuff you're sitting on top of," Snake explained, while Prometheus remained dim and silent. "It's the souls of the less agitated animals of your world."

Thom gazed down through the shimmering ocean beneath his cloud. "That's made of animal souls?"

"Yes," Prometheus said, his tarnish receding. "Their willpower is strong but also calm, so they gather into a denser mist of life energy."

Snake said, "You're a more scatter-minded soul, so your life energy spreads out, making you lighter. That's why you float."

Thom's cloud grew darker and thinner. None of this made sense. Where was the judgment? Where were his angry ancestors, the pearly gates, the lake of fire, any of it? His thoughts escaping, he muttered, "...and you're not even human?"

Prometheus said, "No, we are not human because we're not of your world."

"We just came to help," Snake said. "But it went really unappreciated. I mean like, Prometheus is Prometheus."

"You mean the liver guy?" Thom asked, remembering an image of Prometheus chained to a rock, a bird eating his liver, an eternal torture for his crime of helping humanity.

"Yes, I gave you fire and was thus depicted as 'the liver guy' as you say."

"And I gave you sex for fun!" Snake proudly declared.

"To be fair," Prometheus said, "you gave that to a lot of species."

Growing a pair of shoulder nubs, Snake shrugged. "I didn't know which one of you would become dominant. To be honest, I was betting on the otters."

Prometheus added, "But we couldn't give your kind anything without it becoming a weapon, sex or fire."

"Yeah, so, he was the actual Prometheus," Snake said, "and I was the actual Snake in the Garden of Eden story. And in Ragnarök."

"But," Thom said, his cloud clenching, "how could both of those stories be true? Which religion is right?"

"Neither story is true, and no religion is right," Prometheus said. "They are merely propaganda fed to your people through surrogates of the soul wells, Alpha and Unum. The wells place words in the minds of your preachers."

"Unum's the big one," Snake said. "But yeah, propaganda. Though I am a snake, kind of."

Certain he heard that wrong, Thom asked, "You're a snake?"

"Kind of," Snake said. "Here, look."

Snake transformed from an orb into a being that looked very much like a snake with a long body of dark brown scales and a diamond head with two nostril slits, two black eyes, and one wide, thin mouth. But unlike any serpent that Thom had ever seen, Snake had four pairs of thin curling tentacles evenly spaced down his body. After a moment, Snake returned to his spherical form. Thom continued to stare.

"Yup," Snake said, "that was me. But in your stories on Earth, I didn't have my coils. I was depicted like the armless snakes of your world."

Still trying to wrap his head around what Snake had been, Thom reluctantly asked Prometheus, "What do you look like?"

Prometheus turned away. "I don't recall."

"I was also Satan in story of Job," Snake declared, "and I was Loki…and also the Monkey King of China. And the Great Serpent that battles Thor, bringing an end to your world. And Prometheus was, of course, Prometheus."

"I was also Lucifer," Prometheus said, "because I tried to raise an army against Unum. I merely failed, giving rise to Alpha."

"But if you hadn't, this whole place would've been wiped out by now," Snake said. "So, don't beat yourself up about it." To Thom, Snake said, "He was also the turtle that your whole planet was supposed to be on the back of. That was a dumb one. Oh, Osiris! He was Osiris in the penis story, but he doesn't like to talk about that one."

"It didn't really happen," Prometheus said, his silver briefly tinting red.

"And yet, you hate it every time I bring it up."

"And yet, you continue to bring it up. It's behavior like this that drove Thor from this planet."

"Wait, Thor?" Thom asked. "The Thor. That kraut—I mean, that German myth?"

"Norse," Snake said. "But yeah, I think they picked up on our little thing we had, Thor and me. But really, we were good friends."

"You intentionally annoyed him until he left," Prometheus said. "The Norse depicted the two of you as destroying their world. It's pretty clear that he did not like you."

"But I liked him."

Prometheus sighed heavily.

"Prometheus was also Casandra," Snake said, "and that time he really was Casandra, the Troy one."

"I was not," Prometheus corrected him. "I spoke to Casandra. I tried to help the people of Troy. Unum had inspired the Greeks to end the Trojans, so their city would no longer feed souls to Alpha, whom they worshiped as the god of…uh…I forget."

Snake said. "So, like you said, Thom, we are Martians, but not from Mars. Does that clear things up?"

No. Nothing was clear. It all confused the hell out of him. With the words of Snake and Prometheus ripping his brain apart, Thom collapsed back into a puddle. He needed to think but he couldn't think. He asked, "Am I in Purgatory?"

"I don't believe we're getting through to him," Snake said.

"This afterlife is not described in any of your religions," Prometheus said. "Well, not exactly, and not in its entirety."

"Yeah," Snake said, "so, Purgatory, Limbo, Siberia…call it what you will. You're nowhere, kid. Does that help?"

It didn't help. Nothing would. Thom could feel his soul losing mass, but not all of it. Why didn't he fade to nothing like Johnston had? He'd been an atheist like Johnston, more so even—Thom had it on his dog tags. So why was he continuing to exist? Why bother?

As his soul became smaller and smaller, Thom heard that voice, the one he knew to be his father, a man whose voice he'd never heard while alive. It said the same thing as before, "I'm sorry, Son. I shouldn't have done that to you."

The words were distant, barely discernable, but Thom definitely heard them. What did they mean? Thom couldn't imagine what his dead father had ever done to him. He died before Thom had learned to walk. He died for his country. But he'd continued the family line. Thom was the one who'd ended it. So why was his dad apologizing to him?

"Hey, Thom," Snake called from somewhere nearby, "I think you know this guy. You should come help him."

Thom's cloud stopped shrinking. The idea of becoming truly nothing felt comforting but it also felt cowardly. Thom couldn't fade, not without finding out what his dad was talking about, and not without facing some kind of judgment.

"Seriously," Snake said, "pull yourself together and get over here, Soldier!"

Thom reflexively gathered himself into a dark cloud, now a quarter the size of Snake or Prometheus. Barely hovering, he drifted over to Snake. There he found a puddle of dark red.

"I got the flare off," said the puddle. "I got the flare off. Did they see it?"

"Corporal Lowenstein?" Thom asked. "Is that you?"

"Sergeant Stoneshield?" said the puddle that was David Lowenstein. "I got the flare off. Did the reinforcements see it? Are they coming? Wait. You're Sergeant Stoneshield. How did you…? You…You're dead. Oh, dear god, I'm dead…"

"Yup," Snake said. "You're as dead as a doornail. But don't let it get you down. I mean, you may be dead but at least you've got a friend."

Floating up behind Thom and Snake, Prometheus said, "That is not always a good thing, having a friend."

"You're talking about me," Snake said. "You're picking on me, aren't you? It took millions of years, but I finally got you to ease up, y' ol' fuddy-duddy."

Prometheus ignored him.

"Lowenstein?" Thom said. "Can you get up, Corporal?"

David didn't answer. His soul darkened and thinned.

"Lowenstein, can you hear me?"

Still, only silence. David's soul was thinning fast. Not thinking, Thom reached out to hold him, as if they were still in living bodies. Two smoke tentacles grew where Thom expected his arms to be. When he touched David, Thom fell into another memory. In it, David was halfway up the ladder when he heard a grenade explode. Through David's eyes, Thom saw his own dying body, face mangled by shrapnel. Peterson lay near him, his leg gone. And Corbin lay face down, blood gushing from under him.

Watching himself die, Thom felt detached. Too much had happened, too many deaths relived.

David got back on mission, hurrying up the metal rungs, not checking for Nazis before throwing himself over the top. Heavy fire focused on him. Grazing bullets tugged at his uniform. A few found their mark, hitting his left arm and shoulder. On his belly, he scurried into a shallow depression. Barely hidden and quickly bleeding out, David got out a flare and fired.

As the flickering light arced across the sky, Thom, who was David in that moment, found himself floating. He'd died but he hadn't figured that out yet. As his soul rose, he gazed out over the open water, searching for reinforcements. The Channel was lousy with Allied ships and landing craft, but none were coming to Pointe du Hoc. The handful of Rangers would have to take the gun emplacements alone. David wanted to get back down there and help them. But he was dead. He'd never make it to Berlin. He'd never find his parents.

With that thought, Thom lurched out of David's memory.

***

Thom was once again a dim cloud hovering above an ocean of shimmering gold. Below him, David's puddle of red grew darker, his haze thinning. Trying to help but falling into that memory instead, Thom only made things worse. He was going to lose David the way he'd lost Johnston.

"Stay with me," Thom begged.

David continued to fade. Thom had to try something else.

"Corporal Lowenstein," Thom barked, "get yourself together, Soldier!"

David's haze thickened slightly. "Sergeant Stoneshield?"

"That's right. Stay with me, Corporal. We'll get through this."

David said, "But you're dead. And I'm dead. And the flare…pointless."

"I know, Corporal, but I need you to stay with me."

"I don't understand. I was on the cliff, then I swear I saw these two giant squids or octopuses or somethings."

"Those were soul wells," Snake said, butting in. "Good thing you got past them."

"But my mom." David's fog swelled. "I heard her in there. My mom was inside one of those things. I think. I don't even know if she's dead, but I heard her. That must mean she's dead. Doesn't it?"

"I wouldn't trust that it was her," Prometheus said, hovering apart from them. "It could've been her, but the soul wells sometimes use echoes of your loved ones to lure you in. The well could've been drawing upon your memories."

"But that couldn't've been a memory," David said, his fog thinning again. "She said she was proud of me…proud that I'd become a soldier. I think my mom died and went to…I don't know. I don't even know where I am. Where am I?"

Thom said, "we're…uh…it's complicated."

"I died." David grew even dimmer. "I forgot my faith, failed my parents, and died. It's over. Everything is over."

"I promise you, everything is not over," Thom said, though he wasn't sure.

Snake said, "You'll have to explain things better than that, if you want to save your friend. Try sharing the memory of meeting us just now. I mean we cleared things up for you, right?"

Snake was right. It wasn't easy for Thom to wrap his head around it all, but they had cleared things up for him. He needed to get through to David, but *that*? He looked at the tentacles of fog that were his arms and hands. One touch could convey it all to David, everything Thom had learned from Prometheus and Snake...in that weird, weird conversation.

So far, Thom hadn't had any control over what memories he'd experienced. It'd always been the other person's death. He didn't need to relive his own. He definitely didn't need to drag David through it. But with David fading, Thom saw no other options.

He focused on his conversation with Prometheus and Snake. Extending an arm of fog, he touched David, and they fell into that strange conversation. When they came out of it, he found David's cloud swelling with fresh red fog. Around them, a few other souls had risen from below, becoming dark puddles across the surface.

"That can't be true," David said. "This can't be the after-life...and you two are Martians?"

"But not from Mars," Snake said. "Here, look." Snake became his original form again.

"But my mom," David said, barely moved by Snake's trans-formation. "I heard my mom."

"Just a trick," Prometheus said. "That was most likely not your mother. That was a soul well. It wished only to capture you."

"Yeah," Snake said, "those soul wells are real jerks."

"God was a lie." David thinned and darkened. "So much suffering for a lie."

"Stay with me," Thom said. "Don't fade on me."

"Why?" David said. "I'm dead. Why not die some more? I was supposed to save my parents, but I didn't. I didn't do anything but die."

As new souls continued to bubble to the surface, Thom searched his brain for something to say to David. But he hardly knew the guy. They'd trained together, drank together, prepared to die together, but that was the only David he knew—soldier David. The David who was a boy looking for his lost parents, Thom didn't know him.

"David?" said one of the new puddles. "Is that Abe's boy, David?"

"Rabbi Cohn? Is that you?" David said. To Thom's surprise, David gathered his vague essence out of the puddle and drifted over to the Rabbi. "It is you. It's me, David Lowenstein. I'm here. Do you know what happened to my parents?"

"Abraham Lowenstein, the mohel, you're his boy," the puddle of dark blue replied. "How are you, David?"

David said, "I'm dead so…not well."

"Good to hear it," Rabbi Cohn said. "Why haven't we seen you at temple?"

"Because my mom sent me away," David said. "She sent me a long time ago."

"That's right. You went to the Americas to visit your mother's sister."

"Not to visit," David said, as his cloud grew thicker and redder. "My mom sent me away…and for good. She didn't tell my dad. She didn't even tell me. I was supposed to meet my Aunt Ester while her ship was in port—just to say hi. But then my mom told me I had to go with her. And that it was my only chance. And that I had to call my aunt *mama*. Then in that purse, I saw our mezuzah. So, I knew. I knew I'd never—" David stopped short, his red cloud swelling and sparking.

"That's right," Rabbi Cohn said. "Your father was so upset. He wanted you to be a mohel. He was very angry with Lida when she told him. You're his son. You belong with him."

"You saw my parents after I was gone?" David asked. "Are they okay? When was the last time you saw them?"

Thom hovered closer. "David, are you alright?"

David turned toward Thom and roared, "Button your lip!"

"Seriously," Thom pressed, "you're a thunderstorm, and I don't think that's good."

"It's not good," muttered Snake as he backed away.

"You must be patient," Prometheus told David. "Your friend had a traumatic death. His willpower is shattered, and so is his mind."

Ignoring Prometheus, David turned to the Rabbi and demanded, "My parents, Lida and Abraham Lowenstein, what happened to them?"

"You're David," Rabbi Cohn said, as if emerging from a dream. "You're Abe's boy. I was on the train with your father."

David swelled further, dwarfing Prometheus and Snake. Flashes of red lightning arced between David's grinding billows.

Snake's silver shell darked to green. He hastened his retreat.

"What's happening?" Thom begged.

"Souls can explode," Prometheus explained as he followed Snake, "killing themselves and others. Your friend is…he might soon…I recommend a safe distance." He backed away faster.

Thom had done nothing while Johnston faded. He ran away as that German boy was squeezed to death. He couldn't fail David like he failed them. Against Prometheus' advice, Thom inched closer.

"You need to cool down," he told David. "For your own good."

"My dad," David yelled at Cohn, "where was he? What train? Was my mom there?"

"Train…" the Rabbi said. "The soldiers came. We didn't know why. They made us go and…" The Rabbi's puddle turned black. "It was a freight train. They made us get on. We all asked each other but no one knew anything, and the soldiers wouldn't tell us. When we were getting off, I saw your father…but then the solders…" Cohn's dark cloud thinned to a haze, barely existing at all.

David's flashing thunderstorm bathed Thom and the Rabbi in red light. "What happened to my dad?" he demanded. "And my mom? Was my mom there?"

"I didn't see…" the Rabbi trailed off, as if his shattered fragments of memory had drifted beyond his reach.

While Thom and David looked on, Cohn's thinning mist swirled on the brink of nonexistence. Thom wanted to do something, but what? His army training flashed field dressings and

41

tourniquets through his mind. All useless. Before Thom could think of anything helpful, the Rabbi swelled back into a shallow pool.

Looking up at David, Cohn said, "Oh, you're Abe and Lida's boy, David. How are your parents?"

David bristled with sparks. Before he could demand any more of Rabbi Cohn, the sound of indistinct hymns rose from the distance. It was the larger of the two black octopus-monsters, Unum. As it cut a dark wake deep in the ocean of gold, its sound grew closer and louder.

"It's the Torah," Rabbi Cohn said.

"It sounds like a Catholic hymn to me, Mr. Cohn," Thom said. "Don't know which one."

"It's *Rabbi* Cohn," Snake corrected Thom, from some distance away. "Rabbi, not Mister. And you should back away, too, Thom."

Prometheus said, "Yes, before the soul well arrives…or your friend explodes."

"They're reading from the Torah," Cohn said. "They must be with God. Come with me, David. We'll find your parents in His presence."

David's cloud rapidly shrank, his sparks dwindling. "Are my parents dead?"

"Come and we'll find out," Cohn said.

"But that's not God," David said, his red smog now smaller and darker than Thom. "There is no god."

"Listen to Abe's son," Prometheus called. "That is not your God or any god."

As the giant orb neared, Thom heard its hymns grow into a thunderous chorus. Still, the words and melody remained too vague to identify.

The Rabbi's blue soul grew thick like soup, pressing a divot into the ocean. "David, come with me," he said. "They're reading from the Torah."

David cried, "What happened to my dad?"

"Oh, you're Abe's boy. How are your parents?" said the Rabbi, then his soul broke the surface and sank.

David plunged a red tentacle into the ocean, reaching for him. Cohn sank fast, but David kept reaching until he caught him. Thom could feel David's mind vanish into one of the Rabbi's memories. David sank to the surface but didn't break through. He hung there like a fishing bobber, with Rabbi Cohn the lure.

Again, Thom wanted to do something, but what? Joining the memory could do more harm than good. As Thom hesitated, a massive black tentacle swept up from below and latched onto the Rabbi. It dragged him down, pulling David under with him. Not thinking, Thom plunged his own tentacle in after David. When Thom caught him, everything went dark.

***

A rumbling and clacking reverberated through the small, enclosed space. People whimpered. Packed in tight, their heavy coats rubbed each other in time with the clicking tracks. Though Thom had never met any of them, he knew them all. They were his synagogue, his shul. He was their Rabbi. What Thom didn't know was where they were going. No one did.

The train stopped. Everyone lurched forward onto each other. No sooner had they recovered than the doors squealed open, revealing more soldiers, ones wearing those new SS uniforms. The officers stood back, while the sergeants yelled, and the corporals pulled the people from the train.

The soldiers herded them down a muddy path, marching them toward what looked like the gate into a prison. The others looked to Thom for answers. Even Abraham, the mohel, came to him asking what was happening. But Thom only knew as much as they did—which was nothing.

Then a corporal grabbed Abe.

"Yes, that one," barked an officer, standing off, away from the grim march. "Is that the mohel?"

Thom didn't know the word, mohel. But Rabbi Cohn knew, so Thom knew it was the man who performed the rite of circumcision.

The corporal shook Abe. "Are you the mohel?"

Abe stood there a moment, eyes locked wide. The corporal shook him again. Finally, Abe nodded.

"Come with me," the corporal ordered.

Abe didn't go so the corporal dragged him away. Another SS soldier shoved Thom forward, ordering him to keep moving. Thom hadn't realized that he'd stopped. With another shove, he started shuffling again.

Up ahead, screams. Mothers and children firing shrill notes into the dark sky. One high pitched squeal rose above them, destroying all other sound. Then the muddy path, the shuffling people, and the prison gate all exploded into a dark mist that morphed into a golden fog.

Thom was Thom again, his dark blue cloud still tethered to David's red thunderstorm by a tentacle stretched thin, Thom's tentacle. Together they tumbled end over end through the animalsphere, no longer attached to Rabbi Cohn or to Unum. Their clouds spun eddies into the golden haze, until their tumble slowed to a drift, with Thom above.

He called down to David, "Where is Mister…Rabbi Cohn? Did we lose him?"

Before David could answer, Unum's massive tentacle rumbled through the gold, rising toward them. Thom frantically swam for the surface, towing David. Thom yelled for David to swim, but he just hung there like an anchor.

The tentacle closed on them. Thom swam faster. His stretching limb threatened to snap. Still, Thom kept swimming. Unum's tentacle reached the top of its arc and swung under them, barely missing David's soul. As it passed, another soul came into focus, Rabbi Cohn, his dark blue blob stuck to the end of the giant black limb.

David screamed to the Rabbi, "What happened to my father?"

Rabbi Cohn called back, "Is that David? Abe and Lida's boy? How are your parents?"

David roared.

Unum's tentacle curled away, taking Rabbi Cohn with it. "Say hello to your father for me!" called the Rabbi.

David roared again and tried to swim after him. "What happened to my dad!"

Thom kept swimming upward, dragging David's tumultuous soul with him. Despite the resistance, he reached the surface and wrenched David up after. Thom's exhausted soul oozed into a blue pool. Beside him, David's hovering red storm pulsed with sparks.

Gradually, David contracted into a small tempest, while Thom swelled back into a low-lying cloud. They hovered together, nearly the same size, but with David's red fog much denser than Thom's translucent blue haze.

"My dad," David said. "What did they do with my dad?"

"They separated him from the others," Thom said, "because he was a mohel. Why would they do that? Do they think he's a doctor?"

"I don't know..." David muttered. "And the children..."

Thom could still hear their screams.

David's soul thinned and sank into a swirling pool, pressing a divot into the gold, threatening to break through again. Thom remembered his platoon sergeant, Williamson. As Thom ascended into this strange afterlife, he saw Williamson, still in his human form, sinking back down. He couldn't leave his men, he'd said. It was the last Thom saw of him. Then later, on the surface, he watched Johnston fade. In the puddle before him, it looked like David was about to fade or sink or both. Thom had to do something.

Instinctively, he reached out but stopped himself before they touched and triggered another memory. He wished he could use a field dressing, a shot of morphine, or anything. But none of that made sense here. There had to be a way to help David in this screwy place. But Thom knew nothing here. He had all the brains of a newborn babe.

"Stay with me, David," Thom said. "We can figure it out together, whatever happened to your mom and dad. Just stay with me."

David's red smog brightened. "I have to find my parents. I have to know what happened."

"But we're dead. And if they're dead, they're probably in one of those things—the soul wells."

"What if they're alive? I have to find them."

"Down there?" Thom wished he could put a reassuring hand on David's shoulder, something to make David feel less alone. "I don't think you can go back. We can't even see the Earth or the living anymore."

"I can kind of see it," David said, looking down. "Faint clusters of light. Cities I think."

Thom gazed through the gold. He saw only blackness. "I don't. You gotta be hallucinating or something."

"I believe him," Prometheus said as he approached. "I can see the Earth, or rather the souls upon it. You will too, eventually. It's not surprising that David can already, since his mind is so focused on the living."

David said, "So I can go down and find out what happened to my parents?"

"Yes, but that doesn't mean it's a good idea," Snake said as he joined them.

"Are you saying it's a bad idea?" Thom asked. "If he goes, can he come back? Does anyone come back?"

Before Thom got an answer, David's pool of red smog broke the surface and sank. Thom shot a tentacle into the gold, but David sank too fast, vanishing into the glimmering depths. Thom froze, still reaching down, staring at the place where David used to be. He'd failed again. He'd lost another one.

"Nice try," Snake said. "It wasn't going to work. That guy was going straight down, no stopping him. But nice try."

"Will David come back?" Thom asked.

"Maybe," Snake said.

"It's unlikely," Prometheus said. "Souls who visit the living rarely return. They usually remain below until they fade."

"On my planet, I knew a soul who went down and came back. When he returned, he…he wasn't who he was before. He was…" Snake trailed off. That dark green tarnish returned but only briefly.

"What happened to him?"

Snake turned away without answering.

"What Snake describes," Prometheus said, "it happened during the rampage of his Armageddon, so what happened to the soul that Snake speaks of, it will not be the fate of David."

"But he's probably not coming back." Thom said as he sank to the surface. "He's gonna stay down there until he's gone. I lost him. I lost David." Thom shrank into a faint blue puddle. "I lost another one."

Chapter 3
Absent Friends

Thom slowly swirled in his puddle. He'd lost yet another soul, dead forever, or at least not coming back. On Earth he'd lost his parents, his best friend, his family's legacy…even himself. After his death, the loss continued—Johnston, that German kid, Rabbi Cohn, and now David.

Thinking about that German kid, Thom wasn't sure what the soul wells did to him, but after that explosion, he was certain that he was as dead as Johnston. Then when David was flashing with sparks, Prometheus said he might explode.

Thom said, "There was this boy. In the memory of his death, he wanted to get himself captured before he had to kill anyone. After I died…"

He didn't need to say anymore. He knew that Prometheus and Snake had seen what Thom had seen, carried to them on those few words. Thom's puddle cloud shivered.

"Don't worry," Snake said. "That weird feeling you get when you send thoughts without meaning to, you'll get used to it."

"And I see from your shared memory that you are still clinging to your living senses," Prometheus said. "You think you are hearing and seeing but you're receiving and perceiving."

"You know, all those pretty colors aren't light," Snake said.

"They are projected emotions," Prometheus spoke over the interruption. "Your mind needs time to adjust. As Snake said, you will get used to it."

"I bet you're smelling stuff too," Snake said.

Thom checked. "No, I smell nothing."

"Then you're progressing," Prometheus said. "But you wanted to know about the soul of the young man."

"Did he really explode?" Thom asked.

Prometheus said, "The boy's soul was very strong-willed, which increased the volume of his life-energy—"

"Life-energy is that cloud-mist stuff you're made of," Snake interjected. "Basically, it is you."

"This abundance of energy made him desirable to both wells," Prometheus continued. "When they fought over him, he was squeezed to a concentrated point until his life-energy exploded. The boy is no more."

Still processing that, Thom muttered, "And David...?"

Snake grew dark once again.

Prometheus said, "David, what happened to him, it could've been worse than the boy. What happened to David, it was like..."

He trailed off and turned his attention to Snake. Snake remained dark and silence. No one spoke or even thought. The moment lingered until, deep below and miles away, two fresh geysers of light spewed up from Europe, a mass death, probably another battle in the war.

Thom could feel the fear and confusion radiating from the newly dead, all muddled together in one glowing column of green. So many dead, soldiers and civilians, maybe whole families, thought Thom. How many other names would this war bury? But Thom couldn't blame the war for the end of his family. The failure was his alone.

As that thought crossed his mind, he heard it again. "I'm sorry, Son. I shouldn't have done that to you."

He gazed toward the words and found that Unum had arrived to harvest souls from the Eastern Front. The smaller one, Alpha, crept up to harvest the Western Front where fewer souls were rising. Along with the mass-fear of the souls, Thom was awash in vague hymns and undulating chimes. Still, he could somehow hear his father.

"Sorry for what?" Thom called.

Prometheus drifted closer. "I wouldn't trust this connection. It could be bait."

"This isn't how bait usually works," Snake said, his color returning to its normal pristine silver. "I mean, the wells are really far away, too far to grab him. And what's that other image?"

"Other image?" Thom asked. As he did, the image coming from his father filled his mind. It was a small man, dressed in formal clothes. Though his face was obscured by the shadow of his fedora and the smoke of his cigar, he seemed familiar.

His dad said, "I shouldn't've left you without someone to guide you."

"Guide me to what?" Thom begged. "I don't understand." Around Thom, the afterlife faded from his perception, while his dad's presence grew stronger.

"I know you don't," his dad said, now looking Thom in the eye. "It's my fault that you don't."

Thom found himself standing on nothing within a void of white. His body was a pillar of fog as tall as a man, and his dad was a disembodied face staring out of the white with two sad eyes. Gradually, his father's face grew a body, one loaded with bulky gear. He was sunk in mud up to his shin. Others were also stuck, all of them soldiers. And out ahead of them, more soldiers racing across Flanders Fields.

A German machine gunner swept side to side, dropping the runners like felling wheat. The gunner's attention turned to the men trapped in the mud, men like Thom's dad. The gun moved methodically from target to target. At the far end, Thom's dad watched the others die first.

Time slowed. As bullets gradually tore apart a soldier three men away, Thom's dad looked him in the eye and said, "I'm sorry, Son. I shouldn't've done this to you."

"Sorry for what?" Thom begged. "What are you talking about?"

His dad looked past him. Thom turned to find Sergeant Gregory Holt standing behind him, his face blank. Thom felt a golden light swell within himself. He asked, "Gregory? Is that really you?"

Face vacant, Gregory didn't answer. This wasn't his soul, merely a memory. Thom felt like a chasm had opened in his chest. Before he could ask his dad why he was seeing Gregory, another figure appeared, that small guy in a suit, his face shrouded by shadows and cigar smoke. And behind the short guy, another person, a young man with reddish brown hair and freckles. Who were they? And why was Gregory here?

His dad said, "If I'd been there, I could've helped you understand."

Thom turned back and saw the slow-motion bullets inching toward the man next to his dad. This would be over soon. Thom was running out of memory. "Helped me understand what? Just tell me, please."

His father didn't answer. He just hung his head. Time sped up to normal. The man next to his dad vanished in a flurry of horror. Then it was his dad's turn. Thom didn't have time to turn away. Thom screamed.

***

Thom lurched out of the memory and back into his hovering cloud body. His thoughts replayed his father's death, the bullets, the blood. Thom tried to stop it, but it kept replaying over and over. Across his cloud, sparks flashed and popped. Pain gripped him like a fist. It felt like he might explode. But finally, the image faded, giving way to thoughts of Gregory and the other two men behind him. The sparks slowly ceased. Thom sank to the surface, becoming a murky blue puddle. Those men, his father's apology, what did it all mean?

The orb of Prometheus hovered over Thom's puddle. "Are you there? Can you speak?"

"I thought I was going to explode but…"

"We thought you'd explode, as well," Prometheus said. "Snake is still afraid to approach. What happened in that memory?"

Thom asked, "Should I share?"

Prometheus abruptly backed away. "You can just tell me…carefully, please."

Thom lifted himself out of his puddle. "I was in Flanders Fields—the First Great War. I watched my dad die. It was horrible…and weird."

"Weird how?" Prometheus asked.

"I didn't see it through my dad's eyes, like in the other memories. I was there as me. And my friend was there, but not him, not his soul. It was my memory of my friend…I think. And my dad talked to me. Kept apologizing. I really don't get why."

Prometheus turned toward the Eastern Front, where Unum fed on the souls rising from the raging battles. "You experienced all of that with your father…and at this distance?"

Cautiously approaching, Snake said, "I don't know what that was, but it wasn't Unum trying to bait you. Something else must be happening. I'm not sure what."

Prometheus said, "I believe you may have some sort of connection to your father, but I've never known of anything like this. The souls in the wells have always been silent, or puppets used to bait loved ones. But your father, it seems to be him, the actual him."

Thom couldn't stop thinking about Gregory and those other men and his father apologizing. Who were they? Why were they there? What could his father have done wrong? None of it made sense. Thom had to make his father explain himself. But first, he had to rescue him from that monster.

"I have to get him out."

"You mean your father?" Snake asked.

Prometheus said, "From the soul well? I don't think that's something anyone can—"

A few yards away, something burst through the surface, releasing ripples far and wide. Then a red sparking cloud swelled like a blister upon the surface. Snake retreated. Prometheus followed.

But Thom moved closer. "David? Is that you?"

"I've been to Hell," said the red storm as it melted into a dark puddle. "The world has become Hell."

"David!" Thom reached for him but pulled back, afraid of the memories he might fall into. "Stay with me, David. Tell me what happened down there?"

"My parents…"

"Your parents? Did you see them?"

"My dad…he's…and my mom…" David's puddle shrank.

Thom couldn't let him fade. He reached out to touch him.

"Stop," Prometheus snapped as he and Snake came closer.

"I have to help him," Thom insisted.

"You'll be pulled into a memory for certain."

"A bad one," Snake added, "a very bad one."

"I need to know what happened down there."

Prometheus asked, "What could you hope to learn?"

"I don't know," Thom said, "but if I'm going to help David, if I'm going to help my dad, I need to know everything I can about this…this…afterlife. I don't know anything. I barely know how to move myself around. I'm a child here, but I need to be a man, a soldier. I can't leave my dad in that monster. I can't stand here and watch David double-die. I must help him. So, I have to know what happened to him down there." Thom reached out for David.

Snake said, "Wait, I'm going with you."

"What? Why?" Prometheus shouted.

Snake said, "Thom is still new to memories—and everything else here. By the look of David, it's going to get ugly in there. I want to make sure Thom makes it out okay."

"Snake, please," Prometheus begged, "It's too dangerous. What if *you* don't make it out?"

Snake said, "Don't worry, it's just a memory. I'll be okay. I promise. And thank you for worrying, my friend."

"I'm doing this," Thom said as he extended a fog tentacle toward David. Snake hovered closer and extended a silver tentacle toward Thom.

"Please, wait…"

But Snake touched Thom, Thom touched David, and all three fell into David's memory of Earth.

Chapter 4
On Earth

Within David's memory, once again Thom was not Thom. He was David. And Snake was David. And David was also David, a version of himself from the past. All three occupied the same mind in this memory. Thom was aware of them, and they were aware of him. Together they plummeted through the animal-sphere as a single entity, falling faster and faster, cutting a downward wake through the golden fog.

As the haze around them thinned, their descent slowed. Thom realized that he had arms with hands and fingers, actual fingers, not just tentacles fashioned out of fog. But they were not his own fingers. They were David's. His body had returned to its human state, even manifesting all the gear he'd had when he died, all but his rifle.

Their descent continued to slow until David's boots softly touched the ground. They stood upon Pointe du Hoc, on the exact spot that David had died. A bitter wind blew in from the channel. Thom had expected to see the invasion still battling along the shore, as had David. Instead, they found empty machine gun nests, burnt out bunkers, and rusting tanks and landing craft.

"What day is it?" asked David the memory. "How long have I been dead?"

"I'm sorry," came a reply.

Memory David turned, taking Thom, Snake, and real David with him. The three now faced an American soldier in full gear, all a translucent grey fog. The solid body of memory David stepped closer to the man of fog. "Sergeant Williamson?"

"I'm sorry I let you die," Williamson said.

"What's happening?" memory David asked. "Did we lose the beach?"

"We lost everything, you and me. We're dead."

"I know. But where's everyone else? Where's the invasion?"

"The invasion?" Williamson thought a moment. "The Ardennes."

David squinted at him. "What's an Ardennes?"

Thom had the same question.

Williamson said, "I can show you."

The cliff they stood upon turned toward land and moved across Europe as if it were a ship at sea. To Thom, it felt like they stood still while the world moved around them. As they sped past hedgerows, farms, and towns, Thom saw the living in their solid Earthly forms, their bodies aglow in emotional light—reds, blues, and greens. And he saw the dead allied soldiers standing silently, staring blankly into the east through translucent eyes, while the Germans stared west, all of them grey.

"How long have I been dead?" the memory of David asked again as the land washed around their cliff.

Williamson turned his sorrowful eyes to David. "It's December."

A chill shot through Thom. It felt like hours, but it'd been months. So much time had passed and what had he done with it? He wallowed in his failures while his dad suffered inside that thing. David had at least done something to help his parents, returning to Earth to find them. Thom had to do something too.

"Why are we here?" asked the real David, while the memory of David became silent and still.

Thom came out of his thoughts and looked around. The memory of Williamson had also become eerily still. The land had stopped flowing around them and the cliffs of Pointe du Hoc had lowered into the ground. Thom was surrounded by the silent ghosts of soldiers, but their gear was old, and their helmets widely brimmed. With drooping faces and dangling arms, the French, English, and American soldiers stared to the east while the Germans and their allies gazed west.

"This wasn't what happened when I went down," the real David said.

"Well, I didn't bring us here," Snake said.

Looking around, Thom couldn't deny it. Though the trenches were filled in, he could still see their shallow depressions ambling across the landscape, barbed wire sprouting here and there like rusty weeds. From the remains of the sandbags that had once protected the machine gun nest, there now grew poppies.

Thom looked at his feet. Though the mud had dried back into dirt, he recognized the spot where his father had been trapped.

"This is where my dad died. I don't know how I did it, but I brought us here."

Thom glanced around, hoping to see his dad or Gregory again but it was only the landscape and ghosts.

"Who's Gregory?" Snake asked.

"How do you know that name?"

Snake said, "You just filled our heads with it. We're all in the same head, remember."

"Oh, yeah," Thom said. "Gregory was Sergeant Gregory Holt, the closest thing I ever had to a brother."

"Interesting," Snake said.

A concept radiated from Snake, something that made no sense to Thom. He wanted to glare at Snake, but Thom was Snake, and they were both David, which made glaring at each other impossible. "What do you mean by interesting?"

"Maybe I should've said 'obvious' instead?"

"What's obvious?" Thom demanded.

"You and Sergeant Holt, of course. You do understand the whole thing between the two of you…oh wait, you don't understand, do you? Oh my."

Thom didn't get what Snake was talking about. Of course, it's obvious. Of course, Thom understands. He flat-out said it: they were like brothers. But this other thing…this radiating concept Thom felt inside his head…it and Snake made no sense.

David snapped, "This isn't why we're here. I have to show you what I saw."

The cliffs of Pointe du Hoc rose out of the dirt and moved across the land again. It brought them to the Ardennes Forest.

The cliff lowered onto the crest of a snow-covered slope. Above them, a canopy of bare branches stretched before a grey sky. Not far down the slope, an American cleared snow from a fox hole. Down the length of the low ridge, other living soldiers did the same. Amongst them, the dead stood staring vacantly eastward.

"Are we on the front lines?" asked the memory of David. "Is this Belgium?"

"They pushed us back," Williamson said. "Fifty miles."

Fifty miles was a serious setback, Thom thought, but they'd made it to Belgium. They'd gone farther than he'd imagined they could in six months.

"But we're in Belgium?" memory David asked.

"This is the front," Williamson said. "But it's not why you came."

"I have to find my parents," David said. "I can feel my father's pain. I have to go to him."

Williamson nodded.

The cliff rose again and carried them through the German lines, into the German cities that had been ripped apart by constant bombing, and then out into the countryside. The cliffs stopped and sank back into the earth. Thom, Snake, and David stood inside the memory of David, beside railroad tracks, gazing down a muddy path to a grim gate. Though far from any battle-front, the stench of death enveloped all.

"My father," said the real David, "he's in there. I can see his sadness."

Within David's memory, Thom could see it too, a blazing inferno of the darkest blue radiating from inside the prison.

The real David cringed from the grim light. "I can't do this again. I can't go back in there."

Snake said, "Yeah, I'm quite okay not going in either."

Feeling David's soul thinning, Thom said, "We can't take him in there, but I need to see what happened. Can I go without you and him?"

"Sure," Snake said, his words quivering in Thom's head. "It's a memory and memories are malleable. But they're not harmless. So, are you sure about this? I mean, I know why I was going to do this—just your standard unresolved issues regarding the death of a loved one thing. But why are you?"

"My dad is in a soul well," Thom said. "I have to get him out. But I have no idea how to do that."

"And you think you'll learn something in there?" Snake asked. "And getting your dad out of a soul well, I don't think it can be done. So…that's a thought."

"Lots of things can't be done until someone does them," Thom said as he glared hard at the grim beacon glowing from the prison. "Sun Tzu said that if you know the enemy and you know yourself, you need not fear any battles. Since I died, I don't know anything about anything. I don't even know what I am anymore. I need to learn everything I can if I'm going to save my dad. Maybe I'll find the answer in there. Maybe I'll find something to help David, or maybe I'll find nothing at all. But I won't learn if I don't go. You can stay here with him, if you want, but I need to do this."

From within their overlapping minds, Thom could feel it weighing on Snake, that memory of whatever had happened to

Snake's wife remained shrouded from Thom; only the emotions escaped, glowing like a pyre in Thom's head.

"Stay here," Thom said. "I'll go alone."

"No…no," Snake said. "I came this far. I need to see this too. David will be okay here."

"Okay. How do we leave him here?"

"He leaves himself here, really." Snake told David, "When we move the memory a step forward, don't come with us."

Thom felt David silently agree.

Together, Thom and Snake stepped the memory of David forward, leaving behind the soul of David. He appeared much like the grey ghosts of dead soldiers, only darker. Leaving his soul standing by the railroad tracks, Thom and Snake walked the memory of David toward the arched entryway through the stone building. Above the arch rose a guard tower. Extending from either side of the arch were fences and barbed wire.

As Thom passed under the arch, he saw fleeting echoes of another memory, one he'd already shared with David, one that had come from Rabbi Cohn. They came as shadows, brief glimpses of families being wrenched apart. Thom realized that this was where the children had been separated from their parents, under this arch.

Thom, Snake, and the memory of David continued forward, passing like mist through the locked gate. Within the prison yard, guards were scattered around the perimeter. They watched over a huddle of whimpering children gathered around a solitary man. The man wore a black suit and a long beard. The children radiated dim tones of green, but the man radiated blue—deep, dark,

63

and cold. This was Abraham Lowenstein, the grim beacon that guided them here.

His hands reached out to the children, trying to soothe them, a hollow gesture from a hollow man. Though Thom and Snake stood yards away, they could feel Abe's thoughts. Abe's mind was trapped in a different moment, the one when this nightmare started.

When Abraham first arrived on that train, a young officer had Abe pulled aside.

"You are the mohel, yes?" the officer had said in German. He was a captain, young for his rank. "Mohel, yes? That means you are good with children, yes?"

This man clearly didn't understand what a mohel was, just that it had something to with children. But regardless, Abe *was* good with children. At least he'd always thought so of himself. Afraid and confused, Abe simply nodded.

"Good, good," said the officer. "Your duty here will be to calm the children. It will be a simple duty and we will give you privileges. Your first privilege is that calming the children is your only duty. Good, yes?"

Unsure what the young man meant by any of that, Abe nodded again.

"Good, good," said the captain, and that was that. He sent Abe off with a corporal.

Now standing amongst the children, Abe heard it, the young officer saying, "Good, good."

He heard it every time he lay down to sleep. Every time he woke. And every time he walked into this yard. He heard it now in David's memory, while the weeping children gathering close, and as Abe tried to hold all their hands at once.

And now Thom heard it too.

"*Gut, gut.*"

As those words continued to play in Abe's mind, the SS Captain appeared at the far end of the prison yard. "The children," he called. "We are ready. Come."

Guards gathered and herded the children forward. Abraham shuffled along with them, muttering assurances that he knew to be lies. He'd said them before, and he'd have to say them again and again.

The children moved slowly across the yard and into a large, tiled room, but not Abraham; a corporal pulled him out before he could enter. While the corporal held Abe back, another soldier slammed the door and sealed it, cutting short the sobbing coming from inside. What happened next released a dark green sphere of emotional energy that hit Thom and Snake like a wall of steel. It threw them out of David's memory, the same way it had thrown David's soul off the Earth and back into the afterlife that surrounded it.

"*Gut, gut.*"

***

"Well," Snake said, "that was...bad."

"Snake!" Prometheus cried. "I thought I'd lost you. What happened in there?"

"The worst thing ever," Snake muttered.

With Prometheus hovering over them, Thom realized that he, David, and even Snake had been reduced to puddles of dark mist.

"Children," Thom said. "You don't want to know."

"Snake, are you okay?" Prometheus begged. "Don't fade on me, Snake."

"Yeah, I'm okay," Snake assured his friend. "I just…I just need a moment."

He began to brighten and gather mass. His swelling body rose from the surface and reformed into a sphere, but much smaller and dimmer than before.

Snake turned to Thom and said, "I thought your civilization was civilized. What the hell is wrong with your species?"

"I don't know," Thom admitted as he drew himself into a low-lying blue cloud. "But those monsters, what they were doing…" He had no words for it. Just thinking about it made him cringe.

Accidentally receiving a blink of memory from Thom, Prometheus shuddered. "I can't believe it either. What *is* wrong with your species?"

Hovering over David's puddle, Snake said, "I think we're about to lose him."

"Corporal!" Thom snapped, like he had before. "Pull yourself together."

But David continued to fade.

"Lowenstein! Snap to it, soldier!" Thom barked in vain.

Prometheus said, "He's beyond the help of encouraging words. There's nothing to be done."

Prometheus was right that words wouldn't help this time. But Thom couldn't standby, doing nothing, while David became

66

nothing. Again, he longed for a med kit and a physical body to use it on.

As Thom's heart ached for some way to help, something deep inside himself glowed gold. The light radiated through Thom's layers of dark blue fog and into David. Bathed in it, David's cloud swelled. Thom hovered closer, feeding him more light. David's soul continued to grow. When David lifted off the surface, Thom expected him to reform into a cloud, floating free. Instead, he circled Thom's cloud, becoming a ring around his middle. Thom kept glowing, feeding light into his friend like a transfusion of willpower.

Snake said, "Wow, I haven't seen that one before."

"Nor I. How are you, David?" Prometheus asked. "Can you speak?"

"My mother," David said, his voice like a distant echo. "She's here, in the afterlife. I know it."

"Rest," Thom said. "Save your strength."

Prometheus asked, "Are you okay, Thom? Is it draining you?"

"No, I actually feel stronger."

"And your cloud has grown," Snake pointed out.

The swirling choir of Nietzsche descended from the sky to rest upon the gold, consuming western horizon. As its dark blue arms slowly swept past Thom, the tips mere yards away, the far-off sphere at the heart of the choir said in a booming voice, "That which does not kill us, makes us stronger."

"I agree," Buddha said from the heart of his swirling choir. His storm descended to fill the eastern horizon, its bright golden arms sweeping slowly past Thom, opposite Nietzsche's dark blue arms.

"At least, in Thom's case, I agree. This experience has given him strength, enough to share."

The swirling red pinwheel choir of Confucius came to join the others, filling the northern horizon with sweeping arms like the others. "Thom's power could help save other souls from fading. This phenomenon needs to be studied and understood."

A massive pillowy cloud of gold filled the southern horizon and declared, "This is truly a new wonder in our sad world. We should celebrate!"

"We have no time for one of your fermented memories, Lao Tzu," Confucius scolded him.

Buddha said, "Thom and David are worthy of much meditation."

"There is no time for meditation or celebration," Confucius insisted. "This could save so many from fading, enough to build an army and defend against the coming of Armageddon. We must work to understand it."

Another billowing golden storm crowded into the north, nudging past the rolling fog of Lau Tzu. The new storm extended a tentacle toward Thom. The limb of fog looked deep into Thom and, without trying, Thom looked back. He saw men in robes, women in flowers, and children running with ribbons. He saw simple monuments made of massive stones, rituals performed in animal skins, and celebrations for the sun. But mostly, Thom saw Druids, like the ones he'd seen in textbook drawings as a child—men in dark robes worshiping at Stonehenge.

"Like the ocean beneath us, you glow with the light of a forest god," said the choir of nature worshipers that Thom perceived as Druids. "You have become one with the soul of an animal."

"Um…" Thom uttered. But his syllable went ignored.

"There's no animal inside Thom," Confucius scoffed. "But I agree that there's something here that must be understood for the good of us all."

"Thom doesn't seem to be on the path to nirvana," Buddha said. "So that's not the source of his light."

"His emotions blow him like the four winds," Lao Tzu agreed. "He is not finding serenity, but his light foretells of good fortune."

"Here's a crazy idea," Snake shouted to the giant choirs, "let's ask Thom how he did it."

As if the thought were his own, Confucius asked, "How did you accomplish this, Thom?"

"I don't know," Thom muttered as he felt the colorful storms closing around him. "I just didn't want my friend to die."

"Interesting," Confucius said. "You wanted to save your friend…very interesting. It would seem this light is Thom's heart, his metaphorical heart, of course."

"Thom's heart has more strength than his size would suggest," Buddha agreed.

"The smallest can be the mightiest of all," Lao Tzu said.

The Druids said, "With this light, Thom could build and lead an army against the coming of Armageddon."

"I could what?" Thom bellowed.

Prometheus hovered closer to Thom and said, "Again, perhaps the one we should ask about this is Thom."

Snake said, "So, Thom, people seem to think you can save lots of souls and maybe even build an army to stop the end of your world. Got any thoughts on that?"

With the choirs pressing in, all Thom wanted to do was shrink out of existence. But he couldn't. The gold coming from inside him felt like a call to duty. To not answer it would be like failing his family name all over again. But he was definitely not whatever "nirvana" was, and he wasn't an animal god either. Thom didn't know what he or this light was. But he knew what he needed to be right now…

"Alone," Thom said suddenly. "I need a moment alone."

"Understandable," Prometheus said.

"I believe we all need a moment of contemplation," Buddha agreed. He lifted away, high into the dark sky.

Buddha's choir remained directly above, but so high it appeared no bigger than a dinner plate. The other choirs drifted off into the distance, where more choirs joined them, cluttering the horizon with clusters different color storms, all intrigued by the phenomenon that was Thom.

"Come along, Snake," Prometheus said. "Let us leave Thom alone with his thoughts."

"Well, as alone as he can be, and I don't mean his David halo," Snake said as he gazed across the stormy horizon. "So, Thom, while you're thinking, be sure to keep David alive, and also come up with a way to save your world and countless others from an infinite cycle of Armageddons, you know, if you can. No pressure."

"Ignore him," Prometheus said as he drifted away.

"What?" Snake said as he caught up. "That's clearly what that gathering of choirs was about, Thom being like a messiah or something."

"He is not a messiah," Prometheus said. "After what you went through, Thom's lucky to still be a soul."

Chapter 5
In Heaven

Thom wanted to drift off somewhere to be alone. But no such place existed here. In all directions, the surface of the animal-sphere was hazy but smooth. There were no hills, no valleys, not even a dent. Thom was trapped by nothing and surrounded by everyone. Buddha, Nietzsche, the Druids, the choirs of the First Great War and the new choirs of the Second, they all hovered in the distance, far off but still there. And David ringed his waist.

He gazed down into what had been the darkness beneath the gold, but it was no longer dark. "I see them," Thom said. "They're faint but I see the living souls now, at least the ones all crowded together."

"Me too," David said, his voice weak but less distant than before. "Just the crowds, like city crowds."

"And I see them on the other side, like the Earth ain't even there." Thom mused, "I wonder if I can see them because I was in your memory...like it's because I went down there, even though it was only your memory."

"I have no idea," David said. "But I know I'm not going back. I can't help my dad, not in that place, and I think my mom ain't even down there. She might be trapped. She saved me from

Germany, but now she's probably trapped. When things started in Germany, I think my mom saw it coming. She sent me to live with my aunt in New York. My aunt was one of those free-thinker types. She'd left the faith before I met her. So, I lived with an atheist for years, and all I became was agnostic. But you became an atheist. Why?"

"Money," Thom said. "The tithings were supposed to be for the church, the community, and the poor. My mom was poor. No one from the church helped us, except for soup. Gangsters gave out better soup. But there's the Pope in the newspaper, silk, gold, jewels. And they give us shit soup."

"I was only nine when I left my parents," David said, "but I'm sure my Temple would've done better than soup. My mom would've done better than soup. I think she organized a banquet a week, and for anything…a bris, Yom Kippur break-fast, Passover Seder, Bar Mitzvah, brit milah, weddings, funerals, homecomings…birthdays for some reason. She just liked people. And that's what I'm getting to. My mom."

"Yeah, she wasn't in your memory. You think she's dead, in a soul well maybe?"

"I think so," David said, his voice sounding stronger, less distant. "Rabbi Cohn didn't know what happened to her. She wasn't on that train. And my dad didn't know either. While I was down there, I found him easy—I felt him from across a continent. But not my mom, not until I was coming back. I think she's inside the big one, Unum. I'm not sure because there's something…weird about it. Like I can feel her existing, like existing a lot, like if I turn around, she'll be standing behind me, but I'm pretty sure she's in that monster."

"I've had the same thing with my dad," Thom said. "But not like that. Have you felt a memory from your mom?"

"No," David said, "but when I got close to Unum, I thought I heard her chatting, like she's enjoying talking to people somewhere. And I swear I heard her say, 'That's my boy, David. Say hello, David.' I thought I'd imagined it. I thought maybe my brain was being goofy. She'd said that to me when I was little, maybe a thousand times. So, it could've been a memory. But I still feel this connection to her, even when those well things ain't around."

Thom said, "While you were down there, I was in my dad's memory of his death. He apologized to me, but I don't get why. It can't be because he died in a war; that's what Stoneshields do. We've been fighting and dying since the Battle of Dunbar when our ancestor, a nobody cart driver named Adam, dragged a dismounted knight behind a boulder, saving him from being trampled. The knight turned out to be an Earl, and he gave us land and the name Stoneshield. My Great Uncle Marv still has our coat of arms with a chip off that stone mounted on it. But I left no one for him to pass it to, no Stoneshield VIII. I'm the last one, and it's my own fault. So why the hell would my dad apologize to *me?*"

Then from somewhere far away, as if whispered across a quiet canyon, his father's voice said, "I'm sorry, Son,"

"Did you hear that?" Thom asked, his cloud swelling.

"Buddha chanting?" David asked. "Yes, I can hear them. They gotta be really loud up there."

"No, not Buddha. I think my dad said…"

Suddenly, Thom found himself to be a person again, wearing his gear from D-Day, and holding his M1 rifle this time. Across a muddy field, Thom saw a familiar machine gun nest. In it, a motionless German gripped the gun while expended brass and belt links hung still in the air beside him. Not far from Thom, an angled cascade of bullets hovered at the ends of widening wakes cut through the misty air. And right in front of Thom, his father stood knee deep in mud, still alive, at least in this part. The men beside him were already dead. Corporal Thomas Jefferson Stoneshield VI would die as soon as the frozen moment moved forward.

His dad broke free of stalled time and turned his wilting eyes toward Thom. "I'm sorry, Son."

"But why are you sorry," Thom begged. "I should be sorry."

His dad shook his head. "No, it was a burden beyond you."

"What are you talking about?"

His dad looked past him. Thom turned. There was Gregory again. Why was he seeing this? He turned back to his father. Before Thom could ask him anything, his dad said, "I have to go now, and so do you."

Time started, and the sweeping bullets closed on Thom's dad.

"No!" Thom screamed and fired his M1 into the German nest.

But his bullets did nothing. They didn't exist here and neither did Thom. Once again, he watched his father ripped apart by flying metal.

Thom fell to his knees in the mud, sobbing. "Why?" he demanded. "Why do I have to see this? Why do you show me Gregory? What is he supposed to tell me?" Thom wiped his eyes. He turned toward Gregory, but he was gone. And his father was gone, and the Germans were gone. Thom knelt in the mud of Flanders Fields, alone.

Looking at the empty holes that had trapped his dad up to his knee, Thom decided it was time to stop blubbering. He pulled himself to his feet and marched over to the empty machine gun nest. Only the trench and barbed wire remained.

"I can't save you here," he told his dad, wherever he was, "and I can't go back and save our family name. But I will save you from that soul well."

As Thom made that promise, the battlefield dissolved around him, leaving only the endless expanse of the golden ocean of Earth's afterlife and the choirs in the distance.

"What just happened to you?" David asked. "You went all blank. Your cloud just hung there, doing nothing, like you weren't in it, or like you were hypnotized or something, only worse because I couldn't feel your brain in there…which is extra weird because now I realize I can feel your brain in there. What the hell is that about? And now that you're back, you're all like this. I mean, look at you."

Thom's fog had become thick like that of the soul wells. He was ball-shaped like Prometheus and Snake. And he was no longer blue. Thom was now a sphere of dark red smog. He still emanated the golden glow, feeding willpower to David. But all else had changed. Thom realized that he looked different outside because he was different inside. Prometheus had said that will-power was everything here. Looking at himself, Thom finally understood.

"I was in that memory again," Thom explained to David, "with my dad, in Flanders Fields, watching him die. But this time, the memory was different. My dad was trying to tell me something. I don't know what exactly, but I do know that he wants me to do something. And the thing I'm gonna do is get him out of that soul well."

"How the hell are you gonna do that?"

Thom confidently declared, "I have no idea."

***

Though the golden light shining from within him continued to help David, Thom couldn't see how he could use it to get his dad out of the soul well. Even if he knew how to teach it to others and they used it to build an army of souls, Thom wasn't sure how that could save his father or fight Earth's Armageddon when it comes. An army without a plan is an army awaiting defeat. Thom needed to learn more before he could come up with a plan for his dad or anything else. He needed to scout his enemy.

The war in Europe had ended. They'd received the news from the few souls still bubbling up from accidents and illness. Unum had moved over the horizon to the Pacific where the other war continued. But for scouting, Prometheus insisted that Alpha was the safer target. So, they traveled over the golden ocean toward South America.

With cities full of glowing souls as his guideposts, Thom led the way. He sped forward with David hung around him and Prometheus and Snake trailing behind. A handful of choirs followed at a distance, ever on the horizon but never behind it.

As they traveled, Thom assessed what he'd learned about the afterlife so far, like which emotions he perceived as which colors. Red was obviously anger, but also stuff like determination. Silver was nirvana, which would help if Thom understood what the hell nirvana was. Blue was sadness, pessimism, and such. Green was generally fear, and gold was generally happiness. But the gold he fed to David wasn't happiness. Thom didn't feel any happiness. He figured his gold had to be empathy; an outpouring of empathy was what kept David alive.

But one thing Thom didn't get about this place was *time*. If it moved consistently for the living, then time was rubbery here—always faster but at different speeds of faster. Thom's only way of knowing how much time had passed for the living was to find out from the newly dead. What felt like hours would turn out to be either days or months.

In the few hours it was taking them to reach South America, how much time was passing on Earth? With no one bubbling up to tell him, Thom had no idea. He'd have to find out later. At the moment, he just needed to get there. Thom sped forward.

From around Thom's waist, David said to Snake, "When we were in my memory of going down to Earth, you were thinking about your wife, but there seemed to be two people. Did you remarry or have a harem or what?"

"No," Snake said. "He wasn't my 'wife' because…"

"He?" David interrupted. "You were married to a guy? Are you a girl?"

Prometheus said, "There are no pronouns in your primitive society to adequately describe Snake's gender or mine."

"We don't have two genders like you," Snake said. "We have one gender. But unlike you and Prometheus, my people need three to make a baby."

"Three parents?" David said. "I can't imagine."

"I know," Snake said, "your species is new. Despite that flexible thinking thing of yours, your species is still nuts."

"You've been advancing quickly but not evenly," Prometheus said.

"And it's had some weird side effects," Snake added.

"Like what?" Thom asked, while still speeding ahead.

"Well, like no one on my planet ever killed anyone for saying that we orbit our star," Snake said. "Your people did figure it out a lot sooner in your history, a couple thousand years sooner, I'd say. But we thought this planet would make you more flexible thinkers than you turned out to be."

"This planet?" Thom asked. "You mean Earth? Why?"

"Your planet has many unusual qualities," Prometheus explained. "Your stable-yet-tilted axis is quite unusual, for example."

"The four seasons thing," Snake explained. "It makes the creatures on your planet more adaptable. My planet always faced our star on the same side. We all lived in the swamp ring that lay between the Vast Sands and the Icy Expanse. I never even heard of a sunset until I came here."

"Then there's your binary, Luna," Prometheus said. "Few planets have tides like yours."

"Luna?" David asked. "Tides? You mean the moon?"

"That's no moon," Snake said.

"The moon is a moon," David said.

"Luna is too large to be a moon, relatively speaking," Prometheus said. "It's your sister planet."

"Okay, whatever," David said. "But your wife or wives, I felt like you were worried that something was going to happen to me, something that happened to one of them. It's been bugging me. What did you think I was going to do to you?"

Snake's shell dimmed. He didn't answer.

After a moment, Prometheus said, "We were concerned you might explode."

Thom stopped and turned to Prometheus and Snake. "You mean like that German kid, the one that got squished?"

"Yes and no," Prometheus said, while Snake hovered silently behind him. "Snake's spouse exploded not because of pressure. It was…"

"It was my planet's Armageddon," Snake interrupted. "The battle of soul wells had ended. One well had consumed the other, becoming our Armageddon. With nothing to stop it, it rampaged through our afterlife devouring all souls and choirs. Then it descended into the world of the living. And it…it…"

Snake paused. His shell dimmed, the silver vanishing under a sheen of dark blue. Thom hovered closer, trying to be there for Snake as he shared this horrible memory. But Thom needed him to keep sharing. As painful as it might be for Snake, Thom needed to know what happened, if he hoped to stop it from happening here.

Thom asked, "Your wife exploded...how?"

"When our Armageddon went down to feed on the living," Snake said. "My spouse, Hasseree, he went down to help them...but he couldn't. And when he came back..."

As Snake trailed off, Prometheus explained for him. "It was the emotional pain. It swelled within him until his life energy reached critical mass."

"Critical what?" David asked.

"Too much energy in one place," Prometheus said.

"Our children," Snake said, his voice distant but inescapable. "He watched Armageddon suck the souls right out of their living bodies. They didn't even know what happened to them. But Hasseree knew. I saw it in his memories when he exploded."

Snake turned and drifted a little distance away. "Hasseree couldn't save them, but he saved me. When he exploded, he threw me off our animalsphere, out into space. I sailed into the void, watching Armageddon sweep across my planet, consuming everything, even the animalsphere. It left nothing but blackness."

"I'm so sorry," Thom said.

"Don't be sorry," Snake said. "Do something. You wanted to watch Alpha so you could come up with a way to defeat it. Let's go do that." Snake turned and sped off toward South America.

Thom quickly followed. "But I'm not trying to defeat the soul wells, at least, not yet."

Snake stopped. "Then what are you doing?"

"Right now," Thom said, "I just want to rescue my dad from that thing. And I don't know enough to even do that."

Catching up, Prometheus said, "I don't know if what you hope to achieve is possible, Thom."

"Yeah," Snake said, his silver slowly returning. "I think you might have a better chance of killing a soul well than stealing from it. You don't pull souls out; they suck you in."

"I have a connection to my dad," Thom said, turning and moving again. "I can sense him inside that Unum thing. I can't save my family's future, but I can save its past. One way or another, I'm getting my dad out."

Snake said, "I don't know what you're going to do, but it's something and that's more than I did for my world…for my Hasseree. I believe in you, Thom. I will be there to help if I can."

"I believe in you too," David said, his ring gaining density. "I think you can do it, save your dad, and then we can save my mom."

"We can do it," Snake said, "the four of us. We can save your dad, his mom, and then maybe kill those things and save the whole world."

"Uh," muttered Thom, "let's just get to South America to start."

With David still around him, Thom got back on mission, racing south. Prometheus and Snake quickly followed. A lot of people expected a lot of Thom. It all seemed impossible. So did stopping the Nazis, but the Allies had done it. They'd succeeded by winning one bit at a time. Thom would win one bit at a time too, starting with saving his dad.

Chapter 6
Know Thy Enemy

They reached South America. The war in the Pacific raged on but had tightened around Japan. On the distant horizon, the massive Unum harvested the rich rain of souls rising from the far-off battlefront. Below them, Alpha harvested few souls, just the normal trickle of human mortality, not the feast of war that Unum currently enjoyed.

Two of Alpha's eight tentacles swept through the gold, collecting the few souls floating up. But its other six tentacles were stretched into long thin threads that reached down into the world of the living. They descended from the animalsphere to touch the surface of the Earth in several places across the southern continent.

Thom asked, "What's it doing?"

"Sipping," Snake said. "And recruiting."

"At the moment," Prometheus said, "it is inspiring the words of the pontificators in your worship centers."

"That's the recruiting," Snake said.

"It's also gathering strength of will from the living souls who pledge their faith to it," Prometheus added. "Their willpower gives Alpha strength, but it's fleeting."

"And that's the sipping." Snake said. "Without that booster, Unum would've overpowered it and become your planet's Armageddon by now. But the important part is the recruiting. The payoff comes when the worshipers die and they head straight for the soul wells, thinking the wells are Heaven, or Valhalla, or nirvana, or whatever. But it's all propaganda. Well, nirvana is kind of real because it's a state of mind, but that didn't stop Unum from turning it into a place instead of a goal. Many Buddhists have been tricked into being Unum food."

Still gazing down, Thom said, "Prometheus, you said that you accidentally created Alpha while fighting Unum. But you were here before people. Did you know Unum before he was a soul well?"

"Unum was one of the first human souls to not immediately fade," Prometheus said as his silver took on a hue of blue. "I befriended him, and I was there when he formed Earth's first choir. Over time, his choir became a large spiral, much like Buddha. But unlike Buddha, Unum had a taste for a choir's willpower. As he drank, his own soul grew darker and darker, until one day, as I looked on, it turned black. The blackness swept through his choir, transforming it into the nightmare that it is today."

"And you helped Alpha fight against it?" Thom asked.

"It was your bronze age," Prometheus said. "I stood alone in the battle, but Alpha had a choir to rival Buddha's. Other choirs joined us, all attacking Unum, all using their arms to whip Unum, trying to break it apart with brute force. But we only hurt the souls Unum had trapped." Prometheus grew a darker blue. "We killed them, burned the trapped souls from existence with our attack. But Unum, the soul well, remained strong."

"That's horrible," David said from around Thom's equator.

"And Snake?" Thom asked.

"I sat it out with Thor," Snake said. "We didn't trust Alpha."

"They were right to not trust him," Prometheus said. "In a desperate moment, Alpha directed the other choirs to merge with his. Most of them obeyed and, almost instantly, it darkened into a new soul well. Then it fed. When it was over, no free souls and only a few choirs were left in your afterlife. So many lost, and nothing accomplished."

"You accomplished something," Snake said as he came closer to Prometheus. "You kept Unum from becoming Earth's Armageddon centuries ago. Without Alpha, this planet would already be dead."

"You bought us time," Thom agreed.

"Time for what?" Prometheus asked, his words plodding.

"Time for me to learn about my enemy. And once I know enough, I will—"

Thom's words stopped short as a blinding green light swept across the afterlife, a light containing fifty-thousand memories, all at the moment of death, all crowding into Thom's mind in a single garbled instant of time. Then the memories and the light faded, replaced by a deep rumbling that emanated from the northern Pacific.

Thom and the others turned toward the sound and saw a pillar of green light rising from the far-off nation of Japan. As it rose, the green displaced the gold. The sudden flood of fresh souls sent violent currents through the golden ocean, flowing away from the phenomenon. Thom watched as the maelstrom enveloped the submerged Unum.

The green pillar continued swelling upwards until it burst through the surface, erupting like a volcano of jade lava. The souls surged over the animalsphere, launching a ring of golden tsunamis across the afterlife. Thom and the others were a whole ocean away, but in a matter of moments the waves would be upon them.

As the swell crossed the Pacific, it grew higher and higher. Below them, Alpha drew in all eight tentacles and leaned into the building undercurrents. Thom contracted into himself, pulling David in as well. Prometheus and Snake pressed against each other until they became two half-spheres forming a singular orb of dark green.

"Move toward it," Thom ordered, already rushing ahead.

"Are you insane?!" Snake yelled.

"It's growing," Thom said. "Reach it before it gets even bigger."

Thom willed himself forward as fast as he could. Prometheus-Snake followed. The wave closed quickly.

Watching the cresting wall of gold rise over him, Thom thought of that German boy and said, "If that drops on us, it'll crush and maybe explode us. We have to swim under it."

"Are you sure?" Snake asked.

"No," Thom said, then he dove into the animalsphere.

Thom cut a spinning wake as he sank deep into glowing haze. Behind him, Prometheus-Snake drafted along his trail. Below him, Alpha raced away from the wave, now trying to escape. What it ran from was a swirling wall of violent eddies.

"Hold on," Thom told David, then braced himself.

The wall hit. Everything seemed to move in all directions at once—pulling, pushing, ripping, and spinning Thom and David around. Somewhere behind him, Prometheus and Snake urged each other to hold on, their voices fading as the currents swept them away.

Thom pushed forward, trying to reach the far side of the turmoil. Finally, he lurched into stillness. He'd made it through. Looking back, he saw the wall leaving and the wave above cresting. The animal souls crashed back into the ocean, throwing up smaller waves that rolled off into the distance.

With David still in tow, Thom swam back to the surface. As soon as he reached it, he looked for Prometheus and Snake, but he saw no one. Even the choirs had fled. He called out for his friends, but no answer came.

"They had to have made it," David said. "If we made it, they had to have, right?"

Thom didn't have an answer. He would've expected them to be okay, but he was starting to wonder.

Something burst through the surface and immediately split into two, releasing a flash of light that filled Thom and David with a brief memory of terror, one redundant to the terror they'd just experienced themselves.

Coming out of the brief memory, Thom found himself looking at Prometheus and Snake. They were two individual orbs again, but they were both dark green and smaller than Thom had ever seen them—half their normal size.

"Are you two okay?" Thom asked.

"Yes," Snake said. "What the hell happened?"

"It was a mass death," Prometheus said. "Look, they've gathered like a lake upon the surface."

Thom turned back toward Japan to find a vast pool of shimmering green gathered upon the golden ocean. Its base sank deep, the fog beneath it made thicker and brighter by its weight.

Thom told Snake, "Take David."

"What?" said Snake and David together.

"Take him." Forming two tentacles, Thom shoved David off on Snake. "I'll be back."

"Where're you going?" David asked.

"To scout my enemy," Thom said. "There are a lot of confused and frightened souls in that lake. Both wells will want them, and they won't want to share. I'm going to see how they attack each other, so we'll know how to attack them."

"Be careful," Snake said.

"As careful as I can be," Thom said.

Then he dove into the golden haze and swam off, leaving Prometheus, Snake, and David behind.

He swam deep, heading toward the underside of the lake, constantly scanning the glimmering fog for Alpha and Unum. The animalsphere grew denser and brighter, harder to see through. Coming under the lake, Thom could feel the weight of it pressing down. The golden fog became thick and oily. Swimming became labored. He wondered what could've killed so many so quickly.

It had to be a Nazi super weapon of some kind. But why were they using it against Japan? An accident maybe?

Thom found no sign of the wells, but he knew they were near. They wouldn't leave this bounty unclaimed. Then he heard it, the discordant song of indistinct hymns mixed with the undulating tone of bells that rang without percussion.

Gazing down, Thom saw a massive black tentacle rising through the dense gold. Quickly, he dove. It passed over him, stirring and thinning the thick fog as it reached up to harvest souls from the green lake. The first tentacle curled away with its bounty, and another swept in, thinning the haze enough for Thom to see. He watched as the new limb lashed the underside of the lake, grabbing souls from it before vanishing back into the murky depths.

Three more arms swept in, each lapping at the lake, thinning the haze even more. But Thom still couldn't see the giants' heads, only their limbs. He plunged deeper into the gold, following a tentacle carrying a feast of souls back to its mouth. Other arms continued to rise and fall around him. The fog churned with violent currents. The bells and hymns grew louder. Thom pressed on until he emerged into a vast clearing of haze made thin by the whipping limbs. Against the everchanging winds, Thom held his ground and did reconnaissance.

The two octopus monsters hung side-by-side, with Unum dwarfing Alpha. Their outer shells rippled downward to hold them higher in the animalsphere. Thom had seen Alpha doing the same to keep itself deeper. The natural float point for the soul wells had to be somewhere in the middle, he guessed. Keeping themselves deep or shallow took effort. Thom took note of that.

Both wells had turned themselves over, facing their mouths and tentacles up toward the lake. Unum devoured souls with four arms while whipping Alpha with its other four. Alpha fed with two and whipped Unum with six. Still, Unum did more damage to Alpha than the smaller Alpha could inflict. As they thrashed each other, the impacts disrupted their downward ripples, causing the wells to drop. When Alpha got past Unum's arms and slammed it across the mouth, Unum shuddered and sank dramatically.

"The mouth is a weak spot," Thom muttered, taking note of that as well.

While Unum struggled to swim back up, Thom noticed that, unlike Alpha, the downward ripples would stop at the equator of Unum's giant round head and restart after. The cause of the interruption was a river of smog around the equator driven by a spinning, orbiting storm. Though a small storm, it had arms. It was like a tiny choir of Buddha lying flat against the dark surface of Unum. And instead of a silver orb with arms of gold, this was a golden orb with arms of black.

As Thom focused on the storm, it stopped traveling around Unum's middle and focused on him as well. Unum no longer fought or fed. It drew in its limbs and clenched its octopus head-body around the halted storm, apparently in pain. While Unum sank, Alpha seized the opportunity to feast unchallenged.

Thom stayed with the sinking Unum, his focus on that storm. To his surprise, the storm spoke. "Oh, you're David's friend. It's so nice to meet you. Thank you for looking after my boy."

Thom froze. His motionless body quickly floated up as he gaped.

The storm resumed its course around Unum's middle. Unum unclenched and swam back up. Coming within reach of the lake, Unum fed with only two limbs while the other six thrashed the smaller Alpha. Bursts of multi-colored lightning fired from the impacts as the souls on Alpha's surface exploded. Alpha shuddered and sank but kept feasting with every limb it had.

Unum stopped whipping and seized Alpha's arms, pulling them away from the lake of souls. Alpha swam back from Unum, trying to free itself. It wrenched two limbs free and slammed Unum across its mouth. Unum's indistinct hymns became a scream.

Alpha kept targeting Unum's mouth, hitting it again and again. When the end of a tentacle fell in, Unum closed its circling abyss of a mouth, biting down hard on the hapless limb. Alpha's bells frantically rung. It pulled its other seven arms free and beat Unum with all its might. Lightning exploded from the impacts. Thom dodged bolts of electric memory firing into the animal-sphere. But he didn't retreat. He kept watching, gathering intelligence on how the monsters fought.

Unum focused on the tentacle in its mouth, tilting back to pull harder. Alpha pulled too, stretching the limb thin and taut. Thom watched intently until, to his surprise, the tentacle snapped.

Alpha's bells became a shrill buzz. Unum slurped up the broken end, consuming the souls that formed it. The remains of Alpha's severed limb arced away, bleeding souls like smoke. Some freed souls floated up toward the lake above, becoming a part of it. But most faded from existence, almost instantly.

"Souls can be freed from a soul well," Thom gasped. This proved that he could save his father. And Thom had learned so much more than that. He'd learned when and where the soul wells were vulnerable. He'd learned how to hurt them.

Below Thom, the smoke monsters continued to battle, whipping each other as they sank into the murky gold. But Thom didn't follow. He'd learned enough. It was time to withdraw and bring this knowledge back to the others.

As Thom started for the surface, he heard Unum's storm calling to him, again. "It was nice meeting you! Your father says hello. Oh and, Thom, please give David my love."

Baffled, Thom promised that he would and continued his ascent.

Before he reached the surface, it happened again, another mass death, worse than before.

Chapter 7
The Ties that Bind and Break

It started as a twinkling scattered over a city somewhere in Japan, a dark but powerful green cutting through the dense gold fog. Thom stopped and watched it swell and merge into a single light, as if an entire city had fallen into a shared nightmare. A massive pillar of dark green light rose from it, propelling up into the animalsphere. Then came a vibration, deep and widespread, a thunder without end.

Thom turned and desperately swam up at an angle, aligning his trajectory with the surge of currents he knew was coming. He'd never outrun it. He only hoped to ride it out. But no matter what, Thom couldn't let himself die, not now. Every soul, living and dead, depended on him surviving long enough to tell David or Snake or someone what he'd seen, especially that he'd watched Unum devour part of Alpha's tentacle. And it bled souls, including some that didn't fade. It proved that his father, David's mom, and all the other souls, they could be rescued.

Thom kept swimming. The rumbling grew closer and louder, but he couldn't go any faster. The turmoil overtook him, tossing Thom head over heels through the shimmering whirlpools. He couldn't swim. He could only clench up and hope to survive.

As Thom tumbled, the rising column of green came in and out of view. It shot up and burst through the ocean's surface like an erupting volcano. Souls spewed into the sky and crashed back down like a rain of emeralds. The falling souls slammed the surface, launching bolts of green lightning down into the animal-sphere. All around Thom, they fired. Then one struck him, filling him with memory.

Thom found himself in a body again. It was a thick body, dressed in a business suit. He carried a briefcase and a newspaper. He was old but not elderly, just too old for this war. The soul within his old body pulsed with a deep dark blue. He was Japanese and Japan had lost this war. Everyone knew it, but they did not speak of it.

A sound stopped him in his tracks. He gazed into the sky that peeked between the low skyscrapers around him. From high above, a single American plane dropped a single American bomb. The Japanese man knew exactly what this was, and that he was already dead.

Though Thom hadn't known the word before, he knew it now; he said it aloud with an understanding of exactly what it meant to this man in this memory.

"Hiroshima."

The single screaming bomb fell from the sky. It would land blocks away, but Thom as the Japanese man knew that the distance would not save him. Nothing would.

While a deep fear consumed the man, a horrible realization consumed Thom himself. This mass death hadn't been a Nazis accident, like he'd thought. It was America, his country. And why? At least, why again? After the first bomb, the Japanese knew it was over. Maybe the Allies didn't know they'd already won? It didn't matter, not to this man.

The bomb stopped whistling. Silence and burning light consumed the world. Unlike Thom's death, this man did not float. Instead, he and all the others shot into the afterlife at high speed, all wedged together like spawning fish choking a stream. The man didn't know where he was going but he was going there fast. All he could see was green. All he could feel was fear. The green soon parted to reveal a black sky speckled with multi-colored lights. Was this Yomi-no-kuni, the Shinto afterlife? It certainly wasn't what he imagined.

The man started falling toward a tumultuous ocean of gold. Below, he saw glowing green rocks pelting the surface and busting into smoke. A horrific realization struck him; he himself was a glowing green rock, about to hit the surface.

Thom lurched out of the memory and found himself staring up at the multi-colored stars that were really the souls of beings on far off planets. Beneath him, he felt the animalsphere still rolling from the new influx of souls and the tsunamis it caused. But Thom remembered nothing after the bolt hit him, nothing but that man's death, and probably his second and final death, bursting into nothing. Thom hoped the man remained a soul, pooled with the others in the great green lake.

As Thom lay in his own puddle of green, Prometheus hovered into view above him and said, "I am pleased that you did not die."

"Well, you didn't die a second time," Snake said, now coming into view, with David's soul still hung around his middle. "You should've died but Prometheus saved you."

"Really? How?"

Prometheus said, "When I found you, your haze was thin, so I attended to you as you had attended to David."

"He gave you his energy," David said, "like you did for me."

"After some discussion," Prometheus said, "we believe we understand the nature of this light."

Snake sang, "It's the power of caring!"

"Empathy," Prometheus said flatly. "The appropriate term would be empathy. Understanding and caring about the pain of another, and having the desire to intercede, that is where this light comes from."

"Yeah, I figured that out, too," Thom said.

"If not for this empathy light, we would have lost you for certain."

"What happened to you down there?" Snake asked.

"A lot of things," Thom said. "Including, I found out who caused that mass death. I thought it was the Nazis but—"

"Nazis in the Pacific?" David interrupted. "That doesn't make sense. I thought we hit them with something crazy big, like maybe a million bombs at once."

Thom's puddle of green fog grew darker. "I didn't think we'd do something like that to a whole city. *You did?*"

"After Pearl Harbor, hell yeah," David said. "And it was the right thing to do, hitting them with a million bombs."

"One," Thom said.

96

"One what?"

"One bomb," Thom explained. "It was one bomb and it killed everyone in the city. And we did it twice. And they were ready to surrender before the second one."

"So what," David said, his red ring pulsing. "After what they did to Pearl Harbor and everywhere else, they deserved it."

"The man I just watched die didn't deserve it," Thom said. "He was just a guy walking down the street, waiting for the war to be over. He didn't attack Pearl Harbor."

"No, his country did, and we attacked his country back."

Still hung around Snake, David's ring swelled. His red darkened. Thom wasn't going to make him understand, even if he shared the memory of Hiroshima, he wasn't sure David would be willing to understand.

"There was something else," Thom said, moving on. "I think I talked to your mom...I think. It was very weird."

Prometheus hovered forward. "What do you mean you talked to his mother?"

"How?" Snake asked.

"Where?" David demanded.

"I can show you," Thom said. "Where is Unum now?"

Prometheus gestured off toward a dark green glow. Thom gathered himself into a small green cloud and rose from the surface. The glow he saw was the lake, now much larger after the second mass death filled it with new souls.

A mist formed over its surface—the dissipating vapors of many souls fading out of existence together. Some souls bubbled up and out, ascending to join the many choirs lingering above.

Below, the oily green smog pushed deep into the animalsphere, where Alpha and Unum both fed. Neither fought. Instead, they focused on consuming souls as fast as they could feast.

Thom's green cloud turned blue. If he had more time, he could organize a rescue. He'd have to teach the others how to glow empathy into a fading soul to keep it alive, then organize them into a coordinated rescue effort. He could maybe save one now, by himself, if he focused on it, maybe two if Prometheus helped. But he had to stay on mission. He needed to teach others how to fight the soul wells. He needed to save his dad.

"Come on, David, I'll show you where your mom is." Thom flew toward the lake. The others hurried to keep up.

"Are you sure we want to go toward Japan right now," Prometheus asked. "What if it happens again, the one bomb being dropped? Your soul is strong, but I don't believe it's strong enough to handle another wave."

"What does not kill me, makes me stronger," Thom said, quoting that choir.

"I don't think it works that way," Snake said. "In my experience, that which does not kill you, brings you just a smidgeon closer to death."

"If we haven't bombed Japan since I woke up," Thom said, "then we ain't bombing them again. From what I saw in that memory, the war has to be over by now." He glanced back to Prometheus. "Those bombs, this war, all the wars, it's all a part of the fight between the soul wells, isn't it? It's that thing we saw Alpha doing when it was reaching its tentacles down to the living. All this destruction isn't really us, it's them. Isn't it?"

Butting in, Snake said, "Kind of, but not entirely."

Prometheus said, "Yes, your species is a violent one. Wars would've happened on your planet regardless, but many of your wars have been started or prolonged by the propaganda from the soul wells. And this *one bomb* of which you speak does not bode well for your species. The end is not far away."

Reaching the edge of the lake of green souls, Thom stopped. "There," he said, pointing a small blue smoke tentacle down toward Unum. "There's your mom."

They all gazed down into the thick gold haze made thin by the lapping arms of the two giants eagerly feeding upon the underside of the glowing lake. The storm on the equator of Unum's giant round head raced around and around. The storm's golden orb glowed bright, while its black arms rotated around it.

"There," Thom said. "That's her."

"That's my mother?" David asked as it whipped by. "The storm thing, that's my mom?"

Before Thom could explain, the storm halted, facing them. Unum clenched around it and drew its limbs in.

As Unum began to sink, the storm said, "David! Hello! I missed you so much. I met your little friend, Thom, earlier. He's such a nice boy. I'm so happy you have a friend. I've been so worried about you since I sent you the Americas. How's your Aunt Milly?"

"I...don't...know," David said, his ring shrinking. "What...what are you?"

"What do you mean?" Lida asked. "I'm your mother, of course."

Unum's tentacle reached down and nudged Lida, trying to force her to resume her course.

As the oily smog shoved her forward, she said, "Oh sorry, I have to go, David. Go play with your friends and I'll see you later. Nice seeing you again, Thom." She surged forward, back on her course. As she whipped by again, she said to someone, "Nice boy, that Thom."

David muttered, "That was my mom."

"I gathered," Snake said.

Prometheus said, "I have never seen a soul so independent inside a well before."

"Who was she talking to?" Snake asked. "She was talking to someone, right?"

"There appeared to be at least one other soul with free will within Unum," Prometheus said. "And she was conversing with it. This is definitely unusual."

"Yeah, like should-be-impossible kind of unusual," Snake said.

Thom asked, "Who could she've been talking to?"

"Could be anyone," David said, his fog thin, his words ghostly. "She was always a joiner and an organizer. So…I guess, she made friends in there? Is that even possible?"

Snake said, "Before now, I'd've said no, it's not possible."

"You are an unusual species," Prometheus said. "A very unusual species."

"All this weird stuff," Snake said, "something's happening on this planet."

"Indeed," Prometheus said. "First, David survived his perilous journey to Earth…"

"Then the Thom empathy glow thing," Snake interrupted.

"And now David's mother defies the soul well," Prometheus said.

"Also, whatever's up with whoever she was chatting with."

"It would appear that the flexible thinking characteristic of the human species is starting to assert itself," Prometheus mused.

"Yup," Snake said. "This is some widespread weirdness. What's going to happen next? Something with Thom's dad maybe?"

Thom gazed down at the feasting giants and immediately felt his father's presence. Then he heard him speak. "You can do this," his dad said, the words loud and clear. "You are a Stoneshield. You were born for this."

An image filled Thom's mind: a young man in drab clothes, covered in quarry dust, abandoning his cart of limestone to race into a battle where he didn't belong. A knight of his kingdom had been unhorsed and this young cart driver acted without thought, rushing down the hillside, into the sloping valley. He heaved the fallen nobleman and his armor behind a rock. The lowly commoner stayed with the Earl through the back-and-forth cavalry charges until the Scots were driven into retreat. A fortnight later, that cart driver knelt before this Earl and received his knighthood and a small grant of land. That nearly nameless peasant without lineage or kin, a mere boy whose only title had been cart driver, would henceforth be known as Sir Adam Stoneshield of Dunbar.

"I'm sorry," his father said again, his eyes suddenly peering at Thom from under his wide-brimmed helmet. But Thom was not in Flanders Fields this time. He was not anywhere except looking his father in the eye. "I put an unfair burden on you," his dad said. "I'm sorry for that but now I have to do it again. I know you can do this. I believe in you."

With his eyes narrowed and shoulders squared, Thom answered his father with a firm nod.

Then his dad looked away and the vision ended.

Thom came out of his trance with Prometheus in mid-pontification. "A soul inside a well should hardly be a soul at all. It should be at one with the well, physically and mentally, its mind trapped in a looping nightmare while the soul well steals its willpower for itself. But not your mother. She defies assimilation."

Snake said, "She's like a lump of spoiled cheese in Unum's belly. He can't digest her."

"That is an apt description," Prometheus said. "Your mother is Unum's indigestion."

"But in a good way," Snake added.

David's red soul once again swelled around Snake's middle. "So, we're going to do something, right? We're going to save her, right?"

"What do you propose?" Prometheus asked. "I don't believe there is anything we can do. No soul has ever escaped a well."

Thom said, "I saw one well take souls from another."

"What do you mean?" Snake asked.

"I watched Unum eat the tip of one of Alpha's arms," Thom said, as his blue cloud turned red. "Those arms are made of souls, so Unum stole souls from Alpha. And I saw it bleed more souls. Most of them faded away but some lived long enough to join this lake. That means souls can be removed from the wells."

"So, we can save my mom?" David asked, his ring swelling to obscure nearly half of Snake.

"No one has ever saved a soul from a well," Prometheus warned. "I had an army of choirs with me. We attacked them the way they attack each other. And we failed. No one has ever defeated a soul well."

"You tried to kill it by whipping it with tentacles," Thom said. "And you didn't even know where to hit it, I bet. The mouth is the weak spot if you want to hurt them. But I'm not trying to hurt them. I'm trying to rescue one person, my dad." Thom's soul swelled to match Prometheus or Snake, his red fog thick and bright. "I'm going to pick my moment, a time when Unum is alone and weakened by swimming low or high to feed. I'll free my dad from his nightmare loop. Then I'll rip his soul out of that thing, with my own bare tentacles if I have to."

"I'm not sure it works that way," Snake said. "But it does sound…promising."

"The soul wells use memories as traps," Prometheus said. "They use them to draw you in and keep you there. This will not end like you hope."

"Don't listen to him," David said. "You can do this. And after you get your dad out, we'll get my mom next."

"I think it might actually work," Snake said to Thom. "I think you might really do it."

"This will most likely end in Thom joining his father inside Unum." Prometheus' shell grew dark. "As I said, I will miss your soul, Thom."

"No, he will not," Snake said, almost glowing with red like David. "He will not miss you because you're going to succeed. You're going to rescue your father's soul."

"And then my mom," declared David. "We save her next!"

Chapter 8
Shattering the Past

Full of drive and focus, Thom's cloud had become a thick red ball of smoke, almost as large and as round as Prometheus or Snake. He had a plan, or at least an idea of how to rescue his dad. He just needed a vulnerable moment.

It wasn't long before an opportunity presented itself, Unum feeding upon the victims of a natural disaster in Central America, a hurricane most likely. On the surface of the animalsphere directly above Unum, Thom could see the ripples rolling over its oily black shell. Keeping itself submerged that low was clearly difficult. Opening its vortex-mouth to feed also weakened it. Even from this distance, Thom could see Mrs. Lowenstein's river flowing around the equator of its bulbous head, making it even harder to remain submerged. Thom didn't know what she was doing inside that soul well, but she was definitely Unum's indigestion, like Prometheus had said. Under the strain of feeding, submerging, and Lida, Unum's indistinct hymns sounded shaky and forced.

To Prometheus, Snake, and David—who still circled Snake's equator—Thom said, "This is it. This my chance to save my dad."

Snake asked, "Are you sure you want to do this?"

"I am here for you, Thom," David said.

"Sorry," Snake said to David, "but you're not even there for you. Fortunately, I'm here for both of you."

Thom said, "You two take care of each other. I have to do this alone."

"I had an army of choirs," Prometheus said, "but you plan to stand alone. Why?"

"Because I don't know if it'll work," Thom said. "I might die or get eaten by that thing, like you said. But I have to try, because not doing something is certain failure. And I've failed my family too much already."

"Are you sure you don't want to assemble some help first?" Prometheus asked, his attention moving to the choirs who had gathered high above and around them in the distance. They'd come to see what Thom's efforts might yield. Most expected him to be lost to Unum.

"Having help didn't help you," Thom said. He returned his focus to the distant Unum. "It's down there feeding, which means it has its tentacles out and its mouth open. That makes it weaker. Its natural float point is somewhere in the middle of the animal-sphere, so it's struggling to stay down that low. And Alpha isn't around to complicate things. This is my moment. I must do this now. You should all back up because, like I said, I don't actually know what I'm doing, and I don't want to get anyone else killed."

Prometheus backed away and Snake reluctantly followed.

"Don't forget," Prometheus said, "memories are the weapons of the soul wells. When you send your mind into the well, it will try to trap you there mentally as well as physically. Don't let it trap you in a memory."

"I won't," Thom said.

"I know you can do it," David said from around Snake. "My mom is in there, so you have to do this. We have to get her next."

"I'll try," Thom promised. "I'm starting now."

Thom closed his senses to those around him and focused on his father. He projected his thoughts down into the animalsphere, following his connection to his dad. Feeling his father out there, Thom instinctively reached out for him. While Thom imagined reaching a hand out to his father, his cloud body grew a smoke tentacle that reached down into the golden fog, reaching for Unum far below. It kept stretching and stretching, growing thinner and thinner. Thom's fog arm drew out into a long thin thread of red smoke that reached down through the gold and touched the black surface of Unum.

As soon as the thread landed upon the crown of Unum's head, Thom found himself living a memory, but not the one he had expected. There were no soldiers. No machinegun. No mud. Instead, it was sunny. The ground was paved and framed by rowhomes. And there was no one there except Thom. Thom was Thom in his own memory. He wore brown pants, a white T-shirt, and a black eye. He was a little boy and the adult Thom within this memory had no idea why he was here. His dad was long dead before Thom was this age. Coming here made no sense.

His memory-self stomped down the street, his fists clenched, too angry to think straight, too angry to tell adult Thom what this memory was about. And adult Thom kept looking at his brown pants, wondering why they felt significant. Then it hit him, and so did the meaning of this memory.

Young Thom stopped outside his apartment building, looking up at his living room window. His mom was in there. He had to tell her. He didn't want to, but he had to. After the money she'd spent, money they didn't have, money they never had, how could he get himself kicked out of the Boy Scouts?

As he gazed at the window, he remembered how his mom wouldn't be angry, not after Thom explained what happened. But Thom was angry. His mom worked a lot of jobs, sometimes leaving one to go to the next just to keep them fed. Still, she insisted that Thom was going to join the Boy Scouts. Her son was going to have a childhood like all the other kids, the kids with dads. She took on extra shifts at the diner and the grocery store, smiled harder for tips, stayed after to help unload trucks even though she was smaller than the youngest stock boy.

She did all that to give Thom something special, and he threw it away. Why? To stick up for Gil. The skinny, curly haired kid with the perpetually sad blue eyes. Just looking the way he did attracted bullies. He was a good Scout, but it didn't matter. His mumbling and hunching kept getting him picked on. And Thom just couldn't watch it for one more minute.

So, when that jerk, Tim, took Gil's newly earned taxidermy badge, Thom marched to the center of the circle of laughing boys and punched Tim right in the mouth. Tim swung back, catching Thom in the eye. Thom took it and followed with a left jab to the nose. Blood gushed onto Tim's brown uniform. Some even got on the patch. Thom yanked it from Tim's hand and marched it over to Gil, but Gil didn't take it. He just stared wide-eyed at the stiff circle embroidered with a talon, Tim's blood staining its edge. Then Gil ran.

Thom remained there holding the patch, bewildered, until a heavy, adult-sized hand dropped on his shoulder. No one listened to why Thom did it. They didn't care. He'd broken Tim's nose and that was that.

Now, Thom stood at the stoop of his building, looking up at the window, watching his mom's shadow move around the apartment. After all she did for him, all she'd done to get the extra money to send him to Scouts, as if there were such a thing as extra money in this world. What was he going to say to her? How could he explain what he'd done?

Once he got up there, his mom would tell him that he did the right thing and not to worry about the money. But while little Thom was still down on the street, like he was in this part of the memory, all Thom could think about was how he'd failed his mom. Both then and now, his thoughts turned to his dead father and what he would say if he could see Thom coming home, stripped of his uniform.

Adult Thom felt like he'd been failing his family his whole life. And now there was no family. He'd killed it by selfishly acting like a little boy. Instead of starting a family, he wasted his time acting like he was still in the Scouts, still hunting and fishing and living the life of a child instead of a man. Why didn't he get married? Did he even try to meet a girl, ever?

As Thom stood there staring at that window, the sky above it filled with gloom. Someone appeared in the window, but not his mom. It was his dad in his uniform, his face splattered with mud from Flanders Fields. Thom wanted to look away, but he couldn't—he didn't deserve to. He deserved to look up into his father's eyes and think about what he'd done. He killed the Stoneshield name.

The five-storey apartment building faded into nothing, and Thom found himself in Flanders Fields again, with his dad shin-deep in mud. This time, Thom stood between his dad and the machine gun nest. He was an adult again, but he still wore his brown pants and a white t-shirt like on the day he was kicked out of the Scouts.

Thom looked his father in the eyes and said, "I'm sorry, Dad. I was kicked out for fighting."

His father said nothing as he stared past Thom to that machine gun nest. Thom turned and saw Sergeant Gregory Holt manning the gun. He wore the German gunner's uniform. Why did Gregory keep showing up here? And why was he in the machine gun nest about to shoot Thom's dad? What the hell was this all about?

Thom turned back to his father, looking for some kind of explanation. His father met him with unfeeling eyes. Behind his dad, his grandfather stood staring at Thom as well, his eyes equally unfeeling. And behind his grandfather, his grandfather's father, and his father behind him. The entire line of Stoneshield, back to the first Sir Adam Stoneshield of Dunbar, all stood staring at Thom with dead eyes. Their collective gaze weighed upon him like a coat of chains. He looked down in shame.

He'd failed them all.

"No, you haven't," his dad said.

Thom looked up to find the line of Stoneshield patriarchs gone. In their stead, his dad and the other men stood trapped in mud, awaiting the sweep of bullets. Behind Thom, Gregory was also gone, the machine gun nest again manned by Germans. The angled cascade of bullets hung in the air.

His dad begged, "Help me."

Thom's M1 Carbine appeared in his hands. He now wore his uniform with web gear, ammo, and grenades. The inching bullets reached the man next to his dad. They slowly tore him apart. His dad was next. But Thom wasn't going to let it happen like that, not this time. He turned to the machine gunner, aimed his rifle, and fired.

This time his bullet did exist, creeping through the air like the other bullets. Remembering that willpower was everything in this afterlife, Thom willed his bullet to speed up. It broke free of the slowed time and flew at the machine gunner. But it didn't hit the German. It hit the memory itself. As if painted on glass, the false reality shattered, the shards falling away into darkness.

Thom stood on shadows, surrounded by shadows. He was still in his uniform with his Carbine and gear. His father stood beside him still wearing his uniform from the first great war. Someone else was here, too—a memory of someone. Looking past his dad, Thom saw that short slight fellow again, the one dressed in a business suit and fedora. Cigar smoke and gloom obscured his face.

"Who's that?" Thom asked.

His dad smiled. "That's my memory, a very precious one. I really need to explain that. But first, we need to talk about you. I know why you were fighting back then."

His dad gestured. Thom turned and saw his memory of nine-year-old Gil. Just like Thom and his dad, Gil stood in the dark, shapeless void as if there were something to stand on. Before Thom's eyes, young Gil transformed into the adult Gregory.

"I know the real reason you stood up for Gil," his dad said.

"I was trying to do the right thing," Thom said.

"You did do the right thing, but the real reason you—"

"I failed my name," Thom interrupted. "I wasted my life screwing around, trying to do all the things I didn't get to do in the Scouts. I was selfish and immature, and there will never be a Thomas Jefferson Stoneshield VIII because of me. I am so sorry, Dad."

"No, Son, I'm sorry."

"You did your duty to your country and your family," Thom said, tears streaming down his face. "You had me. I had no one. I'm the one who killed our name."

"Thom, you need to listen to me. There's something you must know, and it's not really about you…or your…" His dad's words trailed off as he looked around.

Thom and his dad stood baffled by murmurs now rising out of the darkness. Soon, the shadows filled with hundreds of voices echoing across the nothing, all speaking German. Ghostly grey forms emerged from the gloom, coalescing into people. To either side, tall walls of steel appeared, bowing in as they rose to frame a wide strip of cement, on which Thom and his dad now stood.

Light gathered, illuminating this new space, a busy dock full of German civilians, passenger liners moored to either side.

His dad asked, "What the hell is this?"

Thom shook his head. "I thought it was you."

Chapter 9
A Clash of Giants

Thom gazed at the passing people, their clothes from after the first great war. "Memories are weapons here," he told his father. "This can't be your memory because you were dead before that dress and that hat." He pointed at a passing woman with a high hem line and a Gretta Garbo slouch hat.

His dad said, "Well, we're on a pier for some reason, a German pier."

"That's no memory of mine," Thom said.

"Then whose is it?"

A dark red glow emerged from the forest of people. It moved toward them. It was the shortest and brightest thing on the docks. The crowd parted before it, revealing a little boy holding his mother's hand. Thom had never seen this child before, but he knew him. This was David.

"He must've touched me out there."

"Who did what?" his dad asked.

"That's my friend, David. This is his memory we're in. He must've touched me out in the cloud-afterlife place, bringing his brain inside the soul well with us."

His dad winced. "You're talking gibberish."

"I'll explain better later. Right now, we gotta help him get his brain out of here so I can get your soul outta here."

"You sure that red light is your friend?"

"I can tell it's his soul in that boy."

"How?"

Thom said, "I focused on him."

Thom and his dad turned their focus to David, the soul driving this memory. The details of this day poured into them, as if they'd lived it themselves.

It had been a good day for David. His mom had taken him to a movie and then bought him ice cream. It was still sticky on his face when they arrived at the docks. When David asked what they were doing there, his mom said, "I have one last surprise for you. Your Aunt Milly is passing through and we're going to say hello. She's only here for a few hours but we get to go see the big boat she's traveling on. Isn't that exciting?"

It was 1933 and David was nine so, of course, he was excited. He was so excited that he didn't ask why she hadn't told him sooner or why she was carrying a big black purse for the first time ever. David just wanted to see the ocean liners.

They entered a large but crowded building. Inside it, they passed through customs, showing their papers, saying they had nothing to declare and no ticket to board. Just seeing family, after all. They moved past the little desks with the security guards and soldiers and waded into the sea of people on the other side. All David saw was the midsections of the adults who blocked his view of everything but the ceiling.

Then they stepped outside onto the long, cement pier, where massive ships towered on either side of him. They were small passenger ships in a small port, but they were the biggest machines little David had ever seen. He gazed at them in awe as his mom led him through the crisscross of people.

She led them directly toward two men dressed like soldiers, one new and one old-fashioned. The newer uniform was unfamiliar but the man inside it seemed very familiar, like he and David were friends, and somehow David knew his name to be Thom. And Thom as David knew himself to be Thom. He was looking at himself through David's eyes, while in a memory from moments ago. Realizing this jolted Thom out of David's mind and back into the present moment of this memory, where young David still walked toward him through the crowd.

David and his mom walked directly to and through Thom and his dad. Thom and his dad turned to see David's mom hug a woman standing just behind them. This woman was a stranger to David. But she looked a lot like David's mom—small, thin, with curly brown hair, and projecting an attitude that dwarfed her stature. The stranger also had a big black purse, exactly like his mom's.

After the hug, David's mom bent down and whispered to him, "This is your Aunt Milly, but you should call her *mom*."

David wrinkled his brow and said, "But you're my mom."

"Not today," she said, as she pulled a hanky from her purse. "Today, I need you to call her 'mom,' okay? It's really important. And I need you to go with her on the big boat."

"I don't understand. You're my mom. I don't know her. Aren't you coming?"

"I will," she promised as she dabbed her eyes. "I can't come today. I have to do some things first. But I'll come to you as soon as I can."

"Why can't I go with you?" David demanded. "Why do I have to go with her? Why do I have to call her mom?"

"Shush," his mom said as she drew him in tight. "I need you to be my big man and do everything I'm telling you to do. Things have gotten…complicated. I need you to go with your Aunt Milly to the Americas. I will come as soon as I can get out of Germany, but I have to get you out now."

Tears streamed down David's face. "Why?" he demanded.

"Because I want you to be safe," she said, her tears now flooding past her dabbing tissue. "Things are happening here, grown-up things. I need to get you away from here and then I'll get me and your father out, too. He doesn't see it yet, but I'll make him see it, and we'll do whatever it takes to get back to you. Until then, you need to call your Aunt Milly *mom*. Okay? Can you do that for me? Can you be my big, brave man?"

She was crying. David was crying. Thom was crying. Aunt Milly maintained a smile despite her tear-swollen eyes, while Thom's dad gaped at them all, confused.

"Please," his mom said. "You have to do this for me. If you don't, I could get in trouble. So, can you do that for me, David?"

David looked into her red, dripping eyes. He looked at the gentle smile on Aunt Milly. He looked at Thom and his dad. Then he nodded.

David's mom hugged him hard. Then she hugged Aunt Milly. As they embraced, Thom saw them switch purses. So did David. From him, Thom received another detail from this memory, one yet to come. After David and his aunt boarded, Milly would dig through the big black purse to find papers that said David was her son. The papers were under a bundle of his clothes. Also under his clothes was their mezuzah, the blessing that was supposed to be hanging beside their front door.

The mezuzah's case had been wrapped in a thick ball of yarn, shrouding the Hebrew etched into the brass case. It looked like a muffler waiting to be knitted, but David had recognized the ornate ends protruding from the ball. Seeing it, David felt better. It made him think his mom really would be coming and soon. The mezuzah also told little David that they were never going back to Germany.

But David didn't go to the boat with his aunt, not this David, not this time. Though this David was also a small boy, he stood there, tears pouring down his red cheeks while his mom walked back toward customs, cupping a hanky over her face, and his aunt walked off with the other little David, the one holding his tears in, the one that would get on the boat to the Americas, sailing away from his mom and dad, away from his friends and everything he'd ever known.

But this David, the soul that glowed red, he stood there in the middle of the dock, Thom and his dad standing with him. "Why?" David demanded as he watched his other self board the boat with his aunt. "Why!" he yelled. "Why! Why! Why!" His emotional aura grew past his small body. It's cast a burning red glare across the black painted hulls. "Why!"

The other passengers continued along, unaffected by the little boy who glowed red.

Thom took a step closer to him. "David, it's me. Are you okay?"

"Why?" he demanded through his tears. "Why did she send me away? Why?"

Thom said, "You know why."

David looked at him and yelled, "No!" He yelled it and kept yelling it, his burning light glowing brighter and brighter. The other passengers faded from the memory, but Thom and his dad remained. They leaned into the force of the light as it pushed them, David's roar coming at them like a hurricane wind.

"David!" Thom yelled. "I need you to focus."

David didn't focus. He just kept yelling, "No!"

The winds grew with each cry. Thom and his dad shielded their faces and leaned into the building winds. The gusts pushed them slowly down the dock, their leather soles sliding down the cement pier.

His dad cried, "What in the Lord's name is that?"

Thom looked back and saw a six-foot long, diamond-headed reptile with a thin body and twelve tendril-like limbs. "That's Snake. He's a friend, too."

"*That* is your friend? Where the hell have you been?"

"I'll explain later, but if Snake is in here then something must be going wrong out there. I have to leave this memory right now."

"You can do that?"

"I've done it before," Thom said, though he hadn't, not really. But if he got himself into this memory, he could probably get himself out. "I'll come back and get you out of here. I swear."

"I know you will, Thom," his dad shouted over the rumbling wind. "Just do what you have to do."

With David whipping up a storm and Snake just hanging there, the way out seemed obvious. Thom closed his mind to the memory that surrounded him and focused on Snake. As new memories flowed through him, Thom became a snake-like being crawling through a swampy city with muddy streets, water filled skyscrapers, and electric lights. Thom slithered along a submerged side shelf while the center of the murky thoroughfare was traveled by speeding canoes lined with muck and water. These were Snake's people. Thom had to be inside Snake's memory of his home world.

Almost as soon as Thom realized what it was, it changed. Now he was a flying creature watching its own shadow passing across the tall grass as it glided on a warm breeze. His shadow had a torso and a head, two limbs stretched forward, two limbs stretched back, and broad wings spread wide. The shadow of himself was too distorted by the windswept grass to see more detail than that. Out ahead, he saw a small village of brown domes made of something like wicker. Each had a round entrance at its crest.

This was definitely not Earth, and it wasn't Snake's people either. It had to be Prometheus remembering life on his own planet. Thom wanted to know what Prometheus originally looked like but there were no others of his kind around for Thom to see, none nearby at least. The inhabitants of the village appeared as mere specks in the distance, gliding from dome to dome. Before Thom got close enough to the wicker domes to see the flying creatures in detail, the memory ended.

Thom was Thom again, a red cloud in the afterlife, but he was not on the surface where he'd left himself. He'd been pulled deep into the ocean, where the gold fog now surged around him. Below, Unum battled Alpha. The black smoke monsters ignored the souls still trickling up from the natural disaster in South America and focused on thrashing each other, each using all eight tentacles to whip the other. Where Thom's tentacle touched the top of Unum's bulbous head, the dark clouds swirled up and around Thom's arm, trying to suck him in.

Above, David's ring had extended a tentacle to save Thom from being pulled down. His elongated ring-body still circled Snake. Both hung limp, their minds lost in David's memory of the docks. The only thing keeping them all from being pulled into Unum was Prometheus. He'd extended a tentacle to grab Snake, while spreading his orb body into a wide disc lying flat across the surface of the animalsphere. Though Unum pulled and yanked, it couldn't drag Prometheus under.

Over the discordant bells and hymns of the soul wells, Prometheus yelled down to Thom, "Release your line before we're all pulled in!"

"My dad is still in there," Thom yelled back.

"Your dad is bait! Let him go!"

"No, I can get him out. I need more time."

Prometheus said, "You can throw your own soul away if you want, but you're not taking Snake with you. Let go of Unum or let go of Snake!"

Thom glowed red. "I can't let go of Snake or David, and I'm not letting go of my dad. We can save him. But I need you, Prometheus. Help me. Please."

"Please, Thom, let go. I can't lose Snake. I can't be alone again."

"You won't be alone," Thom promised. "I can—We can do this."

After a pause, Prometheus said, "How?"

Thom said, "I already got my dad separated from that thing mentally. Like he's got his head together in there. Now we need to pull him out physically. Can you pull?"

"I can try," Prometheus said.

Prometheus spread himself thinner and wider across the ocean's surface. Holding tight to Snake with his tentacle, he pulled. Thom's tentacle down to Unum stretched. He could feel his father at the end of his elongated arm, surrounded by dark souls. Prometheus eased off and pulled again, wrenching Snake, David, and Thom upward. A bulge swelled from the top of Unum's giant round head.

Alpha intensified its assault, slamming Unum again and again. Lightning exploded from every impact. The hymns of Unum became a wailing moan. Alpha drew back all eight arms and swung them as one. The impact shot electricity up Thom's tentacle. It filled him with incoherent memories and pain.

Thom was suddenly in the mud of Flanders Fields. Then he was in the boat, watching Johnston bleed to death after he told Thom to get his fucking head down. Then at the docks, leaving David's mother to get on the boat. Lying on his back on the cliff, firing the flare that would bring no reinforcements. In the church parking lot, punching the kid who took Gil's patch.

In the distance, surrounded by the surreal mix of memories, A U.S. Army Ranger walked toward Thom. The soldier clutched a bible with both hands and chanted over and over, "Our Father who art in heaven, hallowed be Thy name."

"Corbin?" Thom muttered at the approaching figure. But it wasn't a question. It was Corbin, the guy who'd been praying with Peterson right before they landed on D-Day.

"I don't have time for you," Thom growled as Corbin came to stand before him. "Where are my friends? Where's my dad?"

"Thy Kingdom Come. Thy will be done," Corbin replied with a sneer.

At those words, a blackness fell over the patchwork of memories, washing them and Corbin away.

Thom found himself in a new memory, or rather a fragment of one. And he wasn't alone in here. Thom was David, and Snake was David, and David was David, and Thom's Dad was also David, all sharing a mind in this memory.

Thom didn't know what the hell was happening in this one, not until his back touched the brick wall. In front of him stood four older boys. They were maybe fifteen while the David in this memory was only ten. They approached, snickering, their silhouettes engraved against the glare of the streetlamp at the mouth of the alley.

One of them drew back a fist, and Thom instantly knew what would come next, because the memory of David knew. There would be pain and humiliation, and this was only the beginning. But then Thom's back touched the brick wall again. And he saw the four silhouettes again, snickering as they approached. One of them drew back a fist and it started again, backing into that brick wall. Over and over, just waiting for the first punch to strike.

This memory had them trapped, just like Prometheus had warned. Unum was wearing them down with one of David's worst memories. And the fragment of time didn't need to be any bigger than this sliver because, when little David's back hit that wall, he knew exactly what these kids would do to him. They'd beat him, strip him, and leave him naked and bleeding in the dark alley. He wasn't their first victim. This was their idea of fun.

From the mind of David, Thom knew what came after this. David would show up on his stoop holding his bare groin in one hand and his bloody nose in the other. Aunt Milly would demand to know who did it.

The next day, Milly took David to track down each of the four teenage hoodlums, and she socked every one of them in the eye. She spent that evening waiting for one of their parents to dare to show up at her door so she could sock them in the eye too. They didn't. She and David spent the next week laughing about what the little thugs must've told their parents, because it probably wasn't that the skinny little Aunt Milly punched them in the face.

But in this moment, when Thom who was the memory of David backed into that wall, it was only fear and pain and no Aunt Milly to exact justice, not yet. This singular moment had adult David and it had Thom's dad and it even had Snake. They were all locked in this loop, too terrified to remember anything else.

Thom fought to keep his sense of self. He needed to think of something before he was lost like the rest of them, no longer thinking, just being the memory. If that happened to Thom too, Unum would be able to pull all their souls into itself, maybe even Prometheus. Thom needed an escape plan.

He knew that this memory went to a place that would be good if they could get there. But they kept looping through the worst part of it, worse than the beating, worse than the stripping of his clothes or the humiliating hobble home. This moment, backing into the wall, watching those silhouettes closing on him, it was worse because he knew all the rest of it was coming and there was no stopping it. And it kept happening over and over, raking Thom's nerves with each reprise.

After this and what Aunt Milly did, the next kid that raised a hand to David got an Aunt Milly right hook to the eye delivered by David, just the way she showed him to throw it. But that David didn't exist in this memory. And David's Aunt Milly wasn't here either. Even if she were, Thom wasn't sure if the memory of Milly could break this loop. And it kept happening, Thom's back, touching that wall, the first punch about to land, Thom's tiny David body clenching and shivering.

If Aunt Milly's soul were here, she'd end this through her own force of will. She wouldn't be trapped, not by this memory. Seeing David like this would propel her into action, Thom was sure. But Aunt Milly's soul probably wasn't in Unum. She might not even be dead yet. Thom needed help from someone like Aunt Milly, someone definitely dead and inside Unum.

As his back hit the wall yet again, Thom realized what he needed to do. He closed his eyes and focused. Ignoring the brick wall, ignoring the silhouettes, ignoring the pain and humiliation about to commence. He ignored it all and focused on being Thom and knowing what Thom knew, not what David felt. With all the willpower he could muster, Thom yelled.

"Mom! David's mom! Help!"

The hoodlums approached again. That fist raised again, ready to strike. But as Thom's back touched the wall, something changed. Thom could feel it. He opened his eyes. Behind the menacing silhouettes there towered a new shadow, eclipsing all beyond the alley. Within it there appeared two eyes that smoldered with grim red flames. Light bled from the burning gaze and crawled over every object in the memory, painting all in tones of fury. Beneath the flaming eyes, a dark void opened. From it boomed the voice of David's mom.

"*Leave my boy alone!*"

The ground trembled. The buildings crumbled. The winds whipped into a roar. Down the center of the alley, the asphalt yawned into a chasm that swallowed the hoodlums, casting their incarnations into nothingness. The bullies were gone but the rest of the memory continued to rumble and rip. The splitting ground spread down the alley until the memory of David himself tore in two, releasing all the souls within.

Coming out of the memory, Thom found Prometheus still spread flat across the surface, keeping them all from being pulled down. David and Snake had escaped the memory with Thom, but still hung limp on the line, half-conscious.

Below Thom, David's mom sped around Unum's equator. She remained gold, but her rotating black arms now glowed red. At the end of Thom's tentacle, Unum's shell swelled like a blister ready to burst.

Alpha slammed its tentacles into Unum, one after another. With each strike, lightning fired into the fog, adding thunder to the ever-rising cacophony of hymns and bells. Despite David's mom and Alpha's whips, Unum tilted back and pulled Thom's arm. Prometheus held on against the giant.

"David?!" Thom yelled. "Are you with me?"

"Mom?"

"No, it's Thom. Your mom is still in there. Are you with me?"

"My mom? I saw her…" His words trailed off.

"So did I. We can save her next, but I need your help with my dad right now. Can you help?"

"I'm good," Snake said, "Well good-ish. But I'm sure you were getting around to asking about me, too, Thom."

Straining to stay above the animalsphere, Prometheus grunted, "Can you save the sarcasm for when we're not in mortal danger?"

Snake said, "No."

"I'm sorry, mom," David muttered. "I'm sorry for being mad." His ring elongated, stretching toward Unum, the opposite of what Thom needed.

Prometheus extended his tentacle around and past Snake, wrapping it around Thom, eliminating the weak link that was David. "I need to inform you that this is extremely painful," he said.

"I know," Thom said, "but my dad's mind is free of that thing. We can get him out. I need you to pull. Please, we almost have him."

"I can help," Snake said as he extended two tentacles, intertwining them with Prometheus' arm, both above and below himself.

Thom said, "On three, everyone pull."

"Everyone but David," Snake said.

Prometheus grunted, "Shut up, Snake."

Ignoring them both, Thom said, "One, two, three!"

Together they heaved. From Unum's northern pole, the bulge swelled. Unum quivered as if in pain. It tilted toward them, easing the tension on Thom's arm. Alpha seemed to be on their side, slamming one tentacle after another across the base of the blister, weakening the clouds that held Thom's dad.

A steady stream of lightning ripped through the animalsphere, dragging thunder behind it. Alpha's bells rang bright, while Unum's hymns became a moan. The collective clamor grew louder and louder while the bulge stretched farther and farther.

Thom, Snake, and Prometheus repeatedly heaved. The black clouds parted and thinned, revealing a tiny blue sphere within. It was Thom's dad, and he was nearly free, but Unum stubbornly held on.

Alpha drew back its tentacles and landed them all in a single slam across the crest of Unum. Lightning exploded from the impact. The hymns of Unum rose into a high-pitched screech. Thom's dad ripped free of the soul well and hurtled upward. The released tension propelled Thom and the others up toward Prometheus as well.

Behind them, a massive lightning bolt irrupted from the rip across Unum's head. It struck Alpha, searing its shell. Its bells rang shrill. Green souls gushed from Unum's wound and quickly overtook Thom. They surged past, up to the surface, tossing the sea above.

When Thom reached the tumultuous surface, Prometheus and Snake no longer had a hold of him. But he still had his stretched-out tentacle wrapped around his father, wherever he was. Thom couldn't see anything but sloshing waves of gold and green. He drew in his overstretched tentacle as he followed it to his father.

When he reached him, his dad was a mere whisp of fog. Despite the sea still tossing them, Thom glowed light into his father. He gradually gained mass. As the waves around them subsided, Thom's dad rose from the surface and gathered around Thom, forming a ring like David had before.

While Thom focused on his father, Prometheus and Snake approached. Both were once again silver orbs. Snake still had David ringing his middle.

"Hey, would you look at that," Snake said as he glowed empathy into David, giving him strength. "I learned your trick, Thom."

Prometheus said, "It appears that the soul wells are retreating."

Looking down, Thom saw the great gash across the crest of Unum still bleeding a trickle of souls as it limped away. While Unum suffered, David's mom seemed fine. She continued to speed around Unum's equator, her soul still gold and orbited by arms of red. Alpha also limped away, baring a broad smoldering gash down its side where Unum's lightning had struck it. Both giants kept their tentacles tucked up tight beneath them as they slowly fled from each other.

Chapter 10
A Gathering Hope

Thom glowed golden light into the ring of fog that was his father, while Snake glowed light into the ring that was David. Around them, many of the newly freed souls faded from existence. Buddha descended and invited the surviving souls to join his choir if they wished. From over the horizon, other choirs came to offer refuge as well. Most joined Buddha, far more than any other choir. They ascended in a slow upward rain of emerald smoke drops. As they merged with the turning arms of Buddha, his choir grew.

Prometheus said, "What shall we call your father? Thom Senior?"

"Should we call you Junior now?" Snake asked.

Thom said, "He's Thomas Jefferson Stoneshield VI. But you can call him Jeff. It's family tradition. The youngest is Thom and his father becomes Jeff. And my grandfather was 'Pop.'"

"That's too complicated," Snake said. "Instead of all that nonsense, I shall call him… *Thom's dad.*"

Feeling his failures welling up inside himself, Thom said, "I would've been Jeff…should've been Jeff. But…"

As Thom trailed off, everyone else's attention was drawn upward. Thom looked up to find the choir of Buddha swelling to dwarf all others. From the orb at its heart, a silver glow emanated out, turning its golden arms to shimmering silver.

"So beautiful," Snake gasped.

Thom asked, "What just happened?"

Prometheus said, "Buddha has become a choir majestic."

"What's that?"

"A big glowing choir," Snake said.

"A thing of great power," Prometheus explained. "It's one stage before becoming a soul well. Alpha and Unum each started as a soul, as did Buddha. Unum and Alpha each gathered choirs unto themselves, then they grew into choirs majestic, then soul wells. Of course, during our war against Unum, the choir majestic stage went by in a blink for Alpha."

"But that's not how its gonna go for Buddha," Snake said. "A choir majestic is still a choir, an entity of many wills bound together by choice. A soul well serves the will of only one soul, with all the other souls surrendering their willpower to it. Buddha would never do that to his choir. It's not who he is."

Prometheus darkened. "I hope your words prove true, my friend."

"Oh, fuff," Snake said. "I know better and so should you."

"I know Buddha is a good soul," Prometheus said. "But I also know that power corrupts. And that is a lot of power."

Snake said, "No matter how big he gets, he will not become a soul well, ever. The real question is what's going to happen with Thom's choir."

"Thom's choir?" Thom asked.

He looked up to find a small collection of souls pooling over him. Thom could feel the identities of those within his choir, the information radiating into his consciousness. They were all veterans, their lives stretching from The Second Great War back to the thirteenth century. As they continued to amass, they formed into spinning arms, like Buddha's. And the space directly above Thom opened, inviting him to become its heart.

"I don't know what they are," Thom said, "but they're not mine."

"What?" Snake asked. "Don't you want your own choir?"

Still glowing gold into his father, Thom said, "I have to focus on him. I don't have time for a choir."

"But it would give you power," Prometheus said, "enough to help your dad. He could become a part of it so they could sustain him. Buddha's choir has saved many in this way."

Thom looked up at the orbiting arms of blue. He could hear them, like a soft chatter coming through a closed door. They had hopes and they'd pinned them on Thom. Some spoke of him like he was a messiah. They all offered him what little willpower they had.

"They can follow me," Thom said, "but I'm not going to be the center of their choir."

"That's quite noble of you," Snake said.

"And foolish," Prometheus said. "That is your power magnifier above you."

"But isn't that the beginning of me becoming another soul well?" Thom asked. He gazed toward the other choirs still gathering souls. "Aren't you worried about me or them?"

"Yes, very worried," Prometheus said. "But you can't hope to stand against a soul well alone. The wells are too strong. You must have a choir."

Hovering nearby, the choir of Nietzsche said, "Those who hunt monsters should be careful not to become them."

Ignoring Nietzsche, Thom said, "I haven't needed a choir so far."

"He did pull his dad out without any help," Snake said.

"No, he had our help," Prometheus said. "He had us."

"And we weren't a choir," Thom said. "We don't need to be a choir to fight together. We only need to be allies."

Snake's silver orb swelled. "I'm with Thom. I think we can do this without him or anyone else becoming a choir. And after what I saw, I don't think he needs a choir...well, not one of his own. Though Buddha could be helpful maybe."

"If I were human," Prometheus said, "if I were compatible with human souls in that regard, I would have a choir."

"Then I'm glad we're not compatible in that regard," Snake said. "It's keeping you from screwing up Thom's plan. And speaking of not being human, I'm really surprised a non-human like me can keep David alive like this. It ain't easy. Kind of hurts, and it's a little itchy too...well, a lot itchy...Okay, it's horrible."

"I had a choir on my planet and..." Prometheus trailed off then said, "It's what you need if you want to save your planet and your afterlife. I cannot see you succeeding any other way."

"Right now," Thom said, "I need to save my dad. But I'm not done with Unum or Alpha. And I'm not becoming a choir."

After the battle to free his father, Thom and the others rested while he and Snake glowed energy into his dad and David. Below them, the Earth glimmered with the new phenomenon of flying people, all stuffed in metal tubes and shuttled about the planet in ever increasing numbers. As more and more aircraft flew higher and higher, the abundance of living passengers became visible, although briefly and faintly.

Then one dot rose above all others. It was bright and green. It continued up through the animalsphere where no living soul had ever been. As it neared the surface of the golden ocean, Thom and the others realized that this bright light was not one but three souls. And these souls were definitely alive.

The souls emerged from the animalsphere, a mere half mile from them, and continued up, vanishing through the mighty arms of the choir of Buddha. Though Thom and the others could see them, the living trio seemed to have no effect on the animal-sphere or on Buddha.

Snake asked, "What the hell was that?"

"And where did they go?" Prometheus added.

"Luna," said the booming voice of Buddha. "They are landing on the Moon."

"It's a planet," Prometheus said.

"Yes," Snake said. "It's a planet. And the humans have managed to reach it?"

"Yes," Buddha said, "there are men on the moon. And they now return."

The three souls fell through the choir of Buddha and back into the animalsphere.

Snake said, "I've never seen technology develop so fast."

"How many planets have you been on?" Thom asked.

"A dozen or so," Snake said. "Most were near their end when I got there."

"I as well," Prometheus said, now watching another trio of living souls rise from the Earth, heading for Luna. "I've seen different kinds of worlds, watched them destroy themselves at various stages of development, always driven toward it by their soul wells. But I've never seen a progression of technology like this. You only just got off your planet's surface and you've already made it to your sister planet, Luna. You're truly a remarkable species."

"It is a moon," Buddha said.

"It's the moon," Thom agreed.

"It's a planet," Prometheus insisted. "And your species is lucky to have it protecting you from meteors and mixing your oceans to create life. It's part of why you are such a remarkable species, and why we had such hope for you."

"That and the titled axis," Snake said. "Your four-seasons thing is horrifying. My people would've died the first winter. If not for Luna, you'd have it even worse with your axis flying all over the place every time Jupiter swung by."

As the vessel carrying living souls returned from Luna to the Earth, another rose in its place, this time passing through Nietzsche instead of Buddha. Around them, other choirs crowded in to watch the living souls traveling to Luna. Thom watched in awe as well, amazed that people made it into outer space. He was glad that he'd lived to see this, sort of. And he didn't care what Prometheus or Snake had to say: the moon was a moon.

As he watched yet another set of souls ascend, Thom said to Prometheus, "I've gotta confess, while rescuing my dad, when I went into that last memory…I wasn't sure you'd keep holding the line. I thought you might let go, or at least let David and me go to save Snake."

"To be honest, so did I. Letting you go would've been the prudent thing. I'm glad that I didn't do the prudent thing."

"Yeah, why didn't you let go?" Snake asked, his silver orb suddenly tinted pink.

Prometheus said, "I honestly don't know."

"Yes, you do," Snake said. "You do know why, and it's because you like me, don't you?"

Prometheus shifted to red. "I don't like being alone, okay? I've spent a lot of time alone. When I left my planet, it wasn't planned. I drifted off on a random course, unable to redirect my momentum. I'd lost everyone and everything and I was lost in nothing going nowhere, and I kept going. Afterwards I always planned my escape before the new Armageddon came. I don't want to drift alone again. I need someone with me, anyone."

"But," Snake said, "you wouldn't've been alone. You're on a planet full of souls. So, I think it was me."

"You?" Prometheus asked.

Snake glistened with an even brighter pink. "You like me."

"If that were true," Prometheus said, "then I could've let David's ring break and just saved you. But I didn't."

"So, then you really like me," Snake said. "You know I would've been furious if you let Thom and David go, so you saved them to be nice to me. You like me!"

Prometheus snapped back to pure silver. His surface solid, clean, and unmoving, he said, "I am not participating in this conversation any further."

Snake turned to Thom and said, "That means he really, really likes me."

"Mom," muttered David's ring of a soul.

"David," Thom said, inching closer to him and Snake. He was careful to not let his dad's ring touch David; neither of them could handle falling into the other's memory, of that, Thom was sure. "David, are you with me?"

His pink receding, Snake increased his glow of gold, projecting more strength into David. Prometheus came closer and, to Thom's surprise, he too emitted a bright glow, projecting it into David and into Thom's dad at the same time.

"David," Thom asked, "can you hear me?"

"Yeah," David said. "Where's my mom and my Aunt Milly? Where am I?"

"You're dead," Snake said. "You've been dead."

"I know," David said, his ring swelling. "I'm not an idiot. We're not in the soul well anymore, right? We're back on the gold. Why is the sky weird?"

"Buddha got bigger," Snake said, as he gestured toward the broad, silver arms now eclipsing most of the sky.

"The higher we soar," proclaimed the choir of Nietzsche from behind Buddha, "the smaller we appear to those who cannot fly."

"Yes," Snake said, "you're bigger too, Nietzsche."

"Where's my mom?" David asked.

"In the soul well," Prometheus said. "She continues to be Unum's indigestion."

David's red ring darkened. "But she was there in the memory with us. Why didn't we get her out?"

Prometheus said, "We were barely able to rescue ourselves and Thom's father."

"But your mom helped," Snake said. "She's quite a personality, your mom."

"And you didn't save her?" David asked, his ring swelling.

"No," Prometheus said, "she saved us, but we couldn't save her."

David's swelling ring unrolled itself from around Snake and reformed into a billowing cloud beside him. "Then what are we waiting for," David said. "Let's go get her."

Snake said, "You can't...or couldn't...even stand on your own...well, not until just now. So..."

"We're not in any shape to mount an attack," Thom said.

"I agree," Prometheus said. "And simply doing as we did before is unlikely to be successful. Unum ignored us, giving us time to extract Thom's dad. After the wound we inflicted upon him, both wells will be sure to defend themselves against us. We must proceed with care."

"Bullshit!" David cried, his red cloud now as large as Thom.

Prometheus flashed red back at him and roared, "It is not bull-shit! We need to recover. Do you not see the state Thom's father is in?"

"I need to help him first," Thom said firmly. "Then we have to figure out how we did this. Then we can save your mom."

Calming but still glowing red, David asked, "That ring is your dad?"

"Yes, and I nearly killed him getting him out."

"Not your fault," said a ghostly wisp of a voice.

"Dad?" Thom asked. "Are you with me, Dad?"

The thin blue ring round Thom gathered mass but remained a translucent haze. "You shouldn't've had that burden."

"What burden?" David asked, his red glow dimming.

"I don't know," Thom said. "I keep trying to apologize for ending our family line, but he keeps apologizing to me."

"I don't get it?" David said. "Did he mean to have more kids besides you maybe?"

"I don't know," Thom said. "But in his memories my best friend, Gregory, keeps showing up. And there's this little guy in a fedora, smoking a cigar. It's like all these neon signs are pointing down a dark hole. I know there's something important down there, but I can't see it. My dad could tell me but...look at him."

"He needs time," Prometheus said.

"He'll get better," Snake agreed. "Just not soon."

"But what about my mom?" David said, his glow rising again. "How are we going to rescue her?"

"Yes, how will we rescue the Mom of David?" asked the choir of Druids from behind the broad arms of Buddha. "Her soul glows gold with her spirit animal. She is ready to be freed."

Buddha said, "What Thom has begun, we must continue if we are to save our world. We must rescue more souls."

"And my mom is next," David demanded.

"Hold on. I only just got my dad out," Thom said. "I'm barely keeping him from fading."

"And it has made you stronger," Nietzsche said from above Buddha.

"It nearly killed my dad," Thom pointed out. "I need to focus on him."

Confucius joined the others and said, "We must examine what Thom has done and learn from it before we act."

"But I didn't do it," Thom said.

"We all did it," Snake said, "together, as friends."

"And my mom broke us out of that memory," David said.

"And your mom helped by beating the stuffing out of Unum," Snake added. "And Alpha actually helped too, though not on purpose."

"And Thom's father separated himself from the soul well," Prometheus said, "a feat I did not think possible."

"And you, Prometheus, kept us from being pulled into Unum," Thom said. "I'm sorry for doubting you."

"No," Prometheus said, "you were right to doubt me."

"Yes, you were right to doubt him," Snake agreed, "but I wouldn't've doubted him. After all, he likes me."

Prometheus sighed.

"It would seem," Buddha said, "that it was not one thing that brought you success, but many."

"Yeah, that's it," Snake said, "you gotta attack the soul wells as a team."

"You also have to know when and where they are weakest," Thom said.

"And you figured that out, already," Snake said.

"Yeah!" David cried. "We know all that stuff, so let's go get my mom!"

"First, we need to meditate on what we've learned," Buddha said, "and what we might have yet to learn."

"I agree," Confucius said. "Real knowledge is to know the extent of one's ignorance."

"Screw you!" David yelled as his red cloud crackled and sparked. "Screw you all! I'm gonna save my mom and I'll do it alone if I have to. Thom, I helped you. Are you going to help me or not?"

Thom looked at the hazy ring that was his father. "I can't. Not until my dad is stronger. I need to focus on him, or he could fade."

"Then screw you, too," David said. "Screw all of you. I'm going to rescue my mom and I'm going to rescue her right now!"

Chapter 11
David's Mom

The simmering red orb that was David sped off, racing toward where Unum had retreated. Still glowing light into his dad's haze, Thom raced after David, followed by Snake and Prometheus. They were four orbs, two solid and two hazy.

Above Thom, his choir continued to center itself over him, while he mostly ignored it. More choirs followed as well—Buddha, Nietzsche, the Druids, and a choir of World War I soldiers, mostly American and British. Other choirs had followed Confucius over the horizon to a safe distance from David's reckless rescue mission.

As they neared Unum, the sound of indistinct hymns rose in the distance. Listening to it, Thom told David, "Rabbi Cohn said he heard someone reading from the Torah, but I hear church hymns, not sure which ones. What do you hear?"

"Someone chanting the Torah," David said without slowing. "Don't know which part and don't care. I'm almost to my mom."

"I don't hear anything," Snake said.

"Because you're not human," Prometheus said.

"I know," Snake said, "but they didn't."

Prometheus said, "The soul wells aren't making any sounds. They're sending out emotional projections as lures. We are incompatible, so we don't hear them like you do."

"But we sense it," Snake said, "like a soft vibration. Really annoying. Makes my nose itch."

"You don't have a nose," Prometheus said. "You never had a nose."

"And yet it itches," Snake said. "I've been on this planet too long."

David stopped. Directly below them, the black orb of Unum fed upon the souls lost in a small disaster or minor war in northwest Africa. And around its middle raced David's mom.

David said, "I don't care if any of you are going to help me or not. I'm going to save my mom."

"I'm in," Snake said.

"I think you should take your time," Prometheus said.

The choir of Buddha said, "You should meditate on what you've learned."

"You need a plan, a real plan," said the choir of World War I veterans.

"Seriously," Thom said, "you don't want to go off half-cocked."

David snarled, "I'm fully cocked and ready to fire."

"I don't think so," Thom said. "Please, listen to reason."

"No."

The choir of Nietzsche said, "Sometimes people don't want to hear the truth because they don't want their illusions destroyed."

"Screw you, Nietzsche," David bellowed up at the billowing blue. "Screw all of you. I am going to save my mom and I'll do it alone if I gotta. The rest of you can all jump in a lake."

"Hey," Snake said. "I said I'm in."

"No, you are not," Prometheus said.

Snake turned his attention to Prometheus. "You finally warm up to me and you immediately start giving me orders. That's so cute."

Prometheus sighed heavily.

Thom couldn't let David do this alone. He said, "Please, just give me some time to deal with my dad, and I'll help you."

"How much time?" David said. "And how do we know how long we've been waiting? It's like I woke up this morning, died, and it's still today. No goddam sun. No goddam moon. And I know time's going faster down there, so every minute we waste is how many hours or days or whatever down there? Prometheus, Snake, do you know?"

"Not a clue," Snake said.

Prometheus added, "The flow of time here seems, in my experience, both fast and inconsistent compared to that of the living."

"Great," David said, "no one knows. I need to do this, and I need to do it now before that thing does something to my mom."

"I don't think Unum is capable of doing anything to your mom," Snake said. "She seems to be kicking Unum's guts around instead."

"If no one will help then I'll just figure it out," David said. "Now are you helping me or not, Thom?"

Thom's sphere contracted. He said, "I'm sorry. My father is barely alive...or existing, I guess. I can't help you. He'd fade."

"Fine. I'm going in now, even if I gotta go in alone."

"I'm in," Snake said again. "I will help you. Me. Right here."

After a pause, Prometheus said, "I will help as well, I suppose."

"Thanks," David said. "I'm going in. Grab me if I sink."

"I'm here for you," Snake said.

Prometheus told Thom, "You stay with your father. We'll help David."

"Thank you," Thom said. "And good luck to all of you."

David focused on his mom. His cloud became still as he extended a tentacle into the gold. As soon as it touched Unum, David went limp. Then he sank into the gold and broke through.

"I got him," Snake said as he wrapped a tentacle around David.

David continued down, dragging Snake to the surface but not under. Prometheus threw a limb around Snake all the same.

"Are you okay?" Prometheus begged.

"I'm good," Snake assured him. "I don't think I need you to hold me just yet...but keep it there anyway."

"I won't let go until you let go of David," Prometheus promised.

Several feet under the surface, David dangled unconscious, his mind lost in a memory. Thom knew it had to be a bad one. He wished he could help, but he had his dad to worry about.

"It's all my fault," said the blue haze that hung around Thom's waist. "I'm so sorry, Son."

"What are you talking about?" Thom begged.

"I knew better," his dad said. "I knew from my own life. I could've helped you."

"I don't understand."

"I'll try to explain." His dad's ring extended a tiny nub in toward Thom and touched him.

Thom found himself in a memory, one of his own, nothing important. Just a good morning on a hunting trip. He sat on a log at the top of a steep slope, looking out over a forest. Mist shrouded all but the tallest trees. A river trickled somewhere beyond sight. From behind him, Gregory walked up and handed him bad coffee in a tin cup. It was barely drinkable. Butthat only made it better because bad coffee was what Gregory did best; bad coffee was Gregory. They sat together in silence, sipping, and looking at the valley.

But then Thom was not Thom and Gregory was not Gregory. Thom was his dad, and his dad was eighteen, sitting on a log, drinking coffee with his friend, Brian, the one with the freckles. Thom's dad put his hand on Brian's shoulder. They looked into each other's eyes. There was something there, something between them. They leaned toward each other, eyes closing.

Thom ripped himself out of the memory.

"What the hell was that!" he shouted. "I mean...I mean...I don't know what I mean but what the hell was that?"

"It's Alpha!" Prometheus cried.

Prometheus had again flattened himself into a disk, forming a flange-like buoy upon the golden ocean. His arm extended down into the animalsphere where it wrapped around Snake, who in turn still held onto the churning red storm that was David.

David's long limb stretched down to Unum. Unum tilted back, trying to pull them under, while Alpha assaulted Unum with all eight of its tentacles.

"We need you," Snake called up to Thom. "I don't know what's happening to David in there, but I don't think he's winning. And I don't think he's found his mom. Can you go in there with me? I don't want to go in alone."

"How could he not find his mom?" Thom asked. "I can see her from here."

"Hello, Thom," called David's mom from far below. "Have you seen my David?"

"And I can hear her from here," Thom added. "…but David is definitely not with her."

"Where's David?" she called. "He's not in his cloud. Is he with you?"

"He's inside Unum," Thom yelled back. "Can you help him?"

"David!" Lida called out. "Where are you?"

"You have to help your friend," said Thom's dad. "He needs you."

"But what about you?"

"We would happily aid your father," said Thom's choir, still hovering above him. "We can shelter him until he can stand alone."

Thom said, "I'm not sure I want him in a choir. In this state, I don't know if he'd ever come out again."

"We can help your father without joining with him," they said. "Leave your father on the surface and we will take care of him."

David needed him. Thom had no choice. He'd have to trust that his choir knew what they were doing. Reluctantly, he formed a tentacle and placed his father upon the surface. Thom's choir descended and covered his dad like a blanket. Together, they glowed nourishing gold into him.

"Okay, I'm going in," Thom said.

"Me too," Snake said.

Prometheus said, "Please, hurry. Holding you all hurts."

From the surface, Thom extended his fog arm down and around David. Almost instantly, he was in the memory.

Once again, Thom was David, and Snake was David, and David was David. They stood on a cement pier framed by passenger liners. Thom recognized it immediately. He'd been here before. This was the memory of David's mom sending him away. Little David—with Thom, adult David, and Snake inside—gazed through tears as his mother made that speech telling him he had to be strong and brave.

The first time she'd made this speech, the time when it wasn't a memory, little David didn't know what was happening or why. But he knew that he had to listen to his mom, that he had to be strong for her. David was only nine, about to turn ten. He wanted to scream and say no, he wouldn't go. But he held onto the promise that his mom would soon follow, that it had to be this way for whatever reason, and he got on the boat.

Now, as an adult, David understood that his mom was saving him from the Nazis, that if he'd stayed in Germany, he'd most likely have died a horrific death at the hands of those who thought he was not human. His mom did it because she wanted to save his life, because she loved him. He understood it all. What he didn't understand was, why did he *hate* her for it?

"You hate your mother," said a voice.

As the last syllable echoed between the hulls, the memory froze. David's mother and every other memory-person on the docks vanished. The hulls changed. In their place were shadowy walls, covered in carvings and ornate stained glass. David recognized it, so Thom did too. It was David's synagogue.

This memory was David's temple, but this wasn't David's memory of it. Someone had hijacked it to use against him, only they weren't getting it right. For one thing, David had never been on the Bimah, he'd been sent away before his Bar Mitzvah. More important, Rabbi Cohn was using his finger to read the Torah, not the silver yad. And his cadence was all wrong.

"Rabbi Cohn?" David asked as he approached, taking Thom and Snake with him. "I know you didn't do this but is that you? Or is that just a memory of you?"

"You were supposed to be a mohel," said that voice, echoing over the Rabbi. "Your father wanted you to carry on the tradition, but you turned your back on God. Your mother wanted you to be safe, but you hated her for it, and you got yourself killed anyway."

Thom looked around, trying to find the memory thief who brought them here. He found only shadows and empty benches. At the pulpit, Rabbi Cohn continued to lay his oily finger upon the sacred scroll, still reading with the wrong rhythm and inflection. The more it went on, the more David wanted to punch someone. Thom and Snake felt it too.

"She saved you from the Nazis," the voice said, "and you ran right back at them. You hate your mother. You, David Benjamin Lowenstein, are a bad son."

"Fuck you," David spat.

"And blessed be to you."

"Wait, I know who that is," Thom said from within David. "Show yourself, Corbin!"

The owner of the voice stepped into the light. It was indeed Corbin. He wore his uniform, clean and pressed, like they hadn't even boarded the ships to cross the English Channel yet. As he pompously strolled into the Sanctuary where he did not belong, David's anger radiated into the memory, bathing all in red light.

"God is calling you, David. He wishes to bring you back to your father and to your faith. You have wandered far, little sheep."

"Don't 'little sheep' me, knucklehead," David snapped. "I don't know if my dad is dead or alive, but I do know my mom is dead and she's somewhere in here. Now give her up or else."

"I can take you to your mom," Corbin said. "Come with me, little sheep."

"That's Catholic stuff, idiot," David said. "Boy, Unum sent the wrong guy to stop me. You don't know my religion, and you don't know memories. My friends and I have been through a couple rough ones, rougher than you. But I didn't come here to mix it up. I want my mom. Now, tell me where she is before I shove this memory up your ass."

Corbin said, "I will take you but—"

151

"Tell me now!" David roared, shaking the memory, and shaking Thom as well.

Corbin staggered back. The synagogue walls became bows of ships. But the customs building and the saltwater beyond either end of the pier did not return. They remained the temple with the Torah at one end and the pulpit at the other, and Rabbi Cohn still reading it wrong.

"Corbin," David shouted, "I don't know what you're doing exactly, but you're bad at it."

"I am showing you the way to the Lord."

Within David, Snake said, "You're not in the lord or with any lord or anything like a lord."

David yelled, "You're in a lie telling lies for a liar. And I ain't gonna listen to them no more. I came here for my mom. Where's my mom?!"

Corbin said, "I will—"

"You will shut the fuck up!" With all his might, David bellowed, "Mom! Where are you? Mom!"

David yelled for his mom and kept yelling. Around Thom, David's memories of the docks and the synagogue mixed, and remixed, the hulls appearing to have stained glass windows. The Sanctuary sank into the cement pier. Incense mixed with the salty breeze.

"Oh, there you are, David," said a calm female voice.

David turned, turning Thom and Snake as well. And there she was, Lida Lowenstein, dressed exactly as she had been on the docks, only without the big purse. She stood there smiling at David. For just a moment, David felt as if he'd never been sent away.

His mom said, "I've been looking for you. But don't be so loud when you're in the temple." She glanced around, more bemused than confused. "At least, some of this is the temple."

David muttered, "Mom?"

"Yes, David?"

"How…? How did you get here?"

"You were yelling for me," Lida said. "So were your little friends, the ones on the outside. They were worried about you. I see you brought two of them with you."

All at once, Thom found himself to be himself again, wearing his D-Day uniform but no gear, and standing next to David, who remained a little boy. On the other side of David, Snake appeared as his snake-like self with four pair of small tentacles evenly spaced down his body. He stood on his four hind tentacles, raising the front half of himself to be a head taller than Thom.

But how had they separated? Had David's mom done it? Had Thom? He wasn't sure.

"It's nice to see all of you," Lida said. "But you should be going now."

David blinked, his mouth agape. "But…I'm here to save you."

She smiled warm and wide. "Oh, David, I don't need to be saved."

Snake said, "You're trapped in a soul well."

"I know," Lida said. "The people here have been helping me understand this place. They're all very nice. I'll have to introduce you later."

David blinked again. "You want to introduce me…later? You want to introduce me to the people you met inside the soul well that you are trapped in?"

"Yes, but not in here. Later, when we get out."

"What do you mean *later*?" David asked.

"We're here to get you out now," Thom said.

Lida shook her head. "Not now. Not me now, anyway. Your other friend needs your help more than I do."

They turned to the other soul who was still in this memory with them, Corbin. He was saying something, but the words never reached Thom. Corbin's mouth just moved in sync with his swinging hands, trying to aggrandize every silent syllable.

Lida said, "That poor boy isn't doing well. You really should take him with you, help him the way you've been helping that other nice man, Thom's father."

David said, "You want me to rescue that jerk Corbin?"

His mother slapped him. "Don't you talk like that. And especially not in the temple." She glanced around at the shifting proportions of port and synagogue. "Well, most of the temple. And I don't care if God is real or not, that's just disrespectful to your father."

"Dad is dead?"

"Yes, but he doesn't know it yet."

"But…but I have to rescue him…and you."

David's mother gently touched his face. "I told you, don't worry about me. And your father doesn't even know he's dead. He needs time. But your friend, Corbin, you need to get him out

154

of this place while you can. Can you do that for me? Can you be my big, brave man?"

Holding her hand, David said, "Last time you said that, I never saw you again."

"That's not true. You're seeing me now."

David's jaw clenched. "You know what I mean."

"I do," admitted his mom, her gaze dropping. "When I made that promise, I really thought I could keep it. But things changed too fast."

"Can you promise me that this time it'll be different?"

His mom hugged him and said, "I want to, but I shouldn't. Instead, I'll promise that I'll do my best to get out as soon as I get everyone together."

"Thank you," David said. "Wait…get everyone together? Who's *everyone*?"

Without answering, Lida vanished from his arms, leaving him on the dock-temple memory mishmash. Corbin's silent voice regained its sound. "—walk with the Lord and he shall show you the way."

Baffled, Thom asked, "Did she say she was saving herself? I mean, that's what she said, right? Is that even possible?"

Snake said, "I think she did say exactly that and, oddly, I think she *can* save herself. So, do we just leave or…?"

"No," David said. "We're not leaving. We have a new mission."

Chapter 12
A Soul's Dark Service

While Thom and Snake looked on, the parts that were the port fell away as the memory of David's temple filled the space around them. Memory David grew into adult David, wearing his D-Day uniform, like Thom.

Corbin proclaimed, "The Lord is my shepherd and—"

David cut him off, saying, "I don't know who taught you to use memories as weapons, but you sure are bad at it. I've been through a few of these. Let me show you how it's done."

David reached for Corbin. Corbin smiled, letting it happen. But Thom grabbed David's hand and pulled it back. "What're you doing?"

"I'm doing what my mom told me to."

"You really want to rescue that guy?" Snake asked. "He's kind of a jerk, ain't he?"

"That's not the point," Thom said. "Doesn't matter that he's a jerk. It matters that he's a trap. Who knows what memory you might get stuck in?"

"Yeah," Snake said, "his soul is only here to lure you in."

"I know he's a trap," David said. "And he's a jerk and he's not why we came here. But he's why we're here now. We came here

156

to get a soul out, so let's get a soul out." He turned back to Corbin.

Corbin said, "You are lost, little sheep. Let me lead you home."

"No," David said, "let me lead *you* home." He reached out to touch Corbin.

This time, Thom didn't stop him.

As David touched Corbin's shoulder, the synagogue transformed into a Catholic church. A pale blue light drifted through the windows barely illuminating the cavernous space. Their ornate glass depicted the Stations of the Cross, something with which Thom was very familiar. His church in rural Pennsylvania had the same scenes in its stained glass. Thom felt strange being in a church again, especially one so like the one he grew up with, a place he thought he'd never return to. It reminded him of the hard times his mom went through, and how little their church helped when they truly needed it. He felt like a justified deserter, returning against his will to corps that didn't deserve his loyalty.

David told Corbin, "I've been through a few of these memory things. Couple of them really did a number on me. I bet being in a soul well is doing a real number on you right now. It did a number on Thom's dad, had him trapped in his own death. Let's see which memory has you trapped."

"I am with God," Corbin said. "Pray and ye shall be with the Lord as well."

"No, you're not with God," Snake said. "You're with a devil…but not *the* Devil…not really."

"Where are we?" Thom asked.

"We're in the church where Corbin served as an altar boy," David said. "He did something bad here, something that really hurt, something he never got over. Let's watch it happen."

The drifting blue light vanished behind a flood of midmorning sun. The door at the back of the church opened, letting in the sound of the congregation socializing just outside. Little Corbin entered, wearing his altar boy red and white silk cassock. Adult Corbin fell to his knees and prayed.

"Our Father who art in heaven, Hallowed be thy name."

The young Corbin peeked outside to make sure no one was coming, then raced down the aisle, passing through adult Corbin.

"Thy kingdom come. Thy will be done on earth as it is in Heaven."

Young Corbin ran up onto the dais and opened the gold doors of the ornate box on the shelf behind the alter.

"Give us this day our daily bread."

From the golden box, young Corbin pulled out the tabernacle wine. From under his vestments, he retrieved a deer hide wineskin and a tin funnel.

"Oh, Corbin," David admonished him, "your savior's blood? You stole the tabernacle wine to be *wine*, not a sacred rite? How could you?"

Eyes squeezed tight, Corbin yelled, "And forgive us our trespasses, as we also have forgiven those who trespass against us."

"And what became of this unholy crime?" David asked. "What came next?"

While the front of the church continued to show little Corbin endlessly pouring the tabernacle wine into his wineskin, the back of the church became Corbin's living room from when he was a kid. His parents were yelling at him, both at once, but the memory had no sound; little Corbin hadn't been listening to the simultaneous scoldings. He was too busy being ashamed.

"You didn't even steal the wine for yourself," David said, shaking his head. "You stole it for some older boys. But you got caught before you even got out of the church."

"Lead us not into temptation!" Corbin yelled, his eyes still squeezed shut, "but deliver us from evil."

David said, "No, Corbin, the lord will do nothing for you. I'll do the delivering from evil. I'm gonna get you out of this memory, then I'm gonna get you out of this soul well."

Snake asked, "What do you want us to do?"

David said, "I have this. You two go. I need you on the outside to pull us out of this well."

"Are you sure?" Thom asked.

David's body, his uniform, and all his gear glowed a blindingly bright red. "I'm sure. But if I get into trouble, I know where my mom is."

"It's hard to argue with David's mom as reinforcements," Snake said as he faded from the memory.

Snake was right. Thom imagined Lida had eyes on her son, even if Thom couldn't sense it. Still, the Sergeant in him felt like he was leaving a man behind. "Alright," Thom said, "but I'll be back if you look like you're in trouble again."

"I won't be. Now go so I can finish this."

Reluctantly, Thom faded from the memory.

When Thom emerged from the memory, he found his cloud body deep in the gold. Above, Prometheus remained a flat disk spread across the ocean's surface to keep from being pulled under. Prometheus held onto Snake, and Snake held onto Thom. Thom had a tentacle around David, who hung limp. David's arm down to Unum was stretched long and thin. Though Alpha slammed Unum with an onslaught of tentacles, Unum focused on pulling David and everyone down.

Prometheus called to Thom, "This is painful...bring this to an end...quickly...please."

Thom said, "David's mind is still in there. And there's been a change of plans. We're rescuing Corbin."

"Who's Corbin?" asked Prometheus.

Snake said, "Some guy they know. It got weird in there."

"Okay, whatever," Prometheus said, his disk body quivering. "Just do something before I can't hold on anymore."

"What do we do?" Snake asked.

"We need to pull," Thom said.

"Then start pulling," Prometheus grunted.

On Thom's word, the three of them heaved as one. Unum's pole tilted toward them. A bulge gathered at its crown like before. Through David, Thom could feel Corbin mentally separate from the collective, but his cloud soul was deep inside, and other subjugated souls were closing around him like a fist. Despite Alpha's relentless attacks, Unum stayed focused on their tug-o-war, pulling hard to drag them down. But Prometheus held.

Thom commanded, "Pull as one, now!"

Together, they heaved upward. Unum's northern cap swelled, ready to erupt. The monster gathered more smog around the bulge, trying to draw Corbin back into itself. Alpha gathered its eight tentacles and swung them as one. Thom expected it to slap across Unum's northern pole, but instead they wrapped around David's arm into Unum and pulled, creating a three-way battle for Corbin's soul.

"This cannot be good," Prometheus said.

"So, do we keep pulling?" Snake asked, his words shaky.

Thom barked, "Yes, dammit! Pull!"

Together, they heaved. Unum leaned back against their efforts. Alpha leaned back as well, pulling against them all. Instead of ripping free like Thom's dad, the green ball that was Corbin's soul gradually emerged from the swirling smog. Thom guessed Unum decided to let go instead of having its head ripped open again, but the well wasn't giving up entirely. As Corbin came free, Unum reached up and wrapped its tentacles around him. Alpha moved its grip to seize the prize as well. Corbin's glowing green soul became the nexus of their three-way tug-o-war. As the competing lines pulled, Corbin glowed brighter and brighter.

"Do not turn your back on the Lord," boomed a new but familiar voice coming from Alpha.

"Is that Corbin?" Snake asked.

"No, it's the other one from my boat," Thom grunted as he kept pulling, "from before I died. The two of them, Corbin and this other guy, Peterson. They were preaching at us. That's Peterson, preaching again."

"Oh," Snake said, "one of those."

From inside Alpha, Peterson called to no one and everyone, "The Lord is the Way and the Light."

Thom said, "I think he's trying to lure Corbin into Alpha."

David's listless, silent cloud body suddenly swelled with red light. As it brightened, David yelled, "Peterson, you bastard!"

Snake said, "David, your mind is back! What happened in there?"

David said, "I got Corbin's brain free. But we gotta get his body free."

"His body is free," Snake said. "Well, free and not free. It's complicated."

"Let the Shepard guide you," Peterson called from within Alpha. "Walk in the light of the Lord."

David yelled, "No, Corbin, don't listen to him!"

Prometheus groaned, "Just let him go. He's not even who we're here for."

"But we're here for him now," David roared. "So, pull!"

"I'm with David," Thom yelled. "We're getting Corbin out. Now, when I count to three, pull, dammit!"

Thom counted and they all heaved upward. Unum and Alpha both leaned back, their black bodies undulating wildly as they swam away from each other. Between them, Corbin glowed even brighter.

"I will fear no evil for You are with me," Peterson called, "Your rod and Your staff, they comfort me."

Prometheus called down to David, "I can't hold on much longer. And you're losing your grip anyway. Just let go."

"We can't give up," David said, his hold on Corbin clearly slipping. "My mom told me to get him out."

"Prometheus is right," Thom said. "This isn't working. And you're about to let go whether you want to or not."

"Shut up and pull! Dammit! Pull!" David tried to get a better hold, but his grip only slipped more. "Mom! I can't hang on! Help!"

From Unum, Lida called back, "I'm coming, Baby Boy."

Unum's tentacle around Corbin suddenly slackened. Alpha hurried to pull the soul toward itself. It kept David from getting a better grip.

Unum shuddered. The tremors centered around Lida on its equator. Her red arms separated from her golden orb and dissolved into the black of Unum. Lightning sparked and popped around her. Then she tore herself free of Unum's body, leaving a broad rip in its black shell. A flood of green and blue souls gushed from the wound she made. Though it was bleeding souls and quivering in pain, Unum held tight to Corbin. Alpha pulled with more ferocity. David's tentacle stretched thin; he screamed in pain.

"I'm coming," Lida called to David.

While the other escaping souls gushed upward, Lida left them and raced toward the nexus of the limbs that held Corbin. Before she got there, David lost his grip and snapped back, sending him, Thom, and Snake surging toward the surface. The soul wells continued the fight over Corbin. They tightened their grips and kept pulling. Between them, Corbin's soul glowed infinitely bright.

Lida turned away from Corbin to follow David and the others to the surface.

"I'm sorry, Mom!" David cried.

"Don't you worry, Baby Boy," Lida called back. "Just get somewhere safe. Quickly please. Oh, and nice to see you again, Thom."

"Nice to see you again too," Thom mumbled, baffled by her politeness in the face of imminent death. He found it perplexing but also reassuring.

Lida said, "And hello to you, Prometheus and Snake. I'm Lida, David's mom. So nice to meet you."

"Uh, nice meeting you too," Snake said, still speeding upward.

When Thom broke the surface, the ocean around him rolled with waves caused by the bubbling influx of souls still bleeding from Unum. Prometheus and Snake had regained their normal silver orb forms. They were now dwarfed by the golden orb of Lida hovering not far above. David had regathered into a cloud of red, as had Thom.

Thom searched the tumultuous sea until he found his estranged choir covering his father like a hen protecting her egg. His dad was safe. After finding his father, Thom gazed down into the gold to see what had happened to Corbin. He found Alpha and Unum still battling for his soul.

They squeezed him harder and harder. Corbin glowed brighter and brighter. Then as Thom expected, he exploded. Like how the German kid exploded when Thom first entered this afterlife, a blinding wall of light fired out from Corbin. Behind the glare, the bells and indistinct hymns screamed in harmonized agony.

Thom braced for the onslaught of memories, but the wall of light never reached him on the surface. It faded into nothing far below. Corbin was gone.

The soul wells were silent and adrift in the gold. Souls bled from the tips of their tentacles, and Unum still bled from Lida's wound. Alpha soon recovered enough to limp away. But Unum remained adrift, as if unconscious. It gradually moved off, carried by a current or maybe momentum—Thom couldn't tell.

He wondered if Peterson had died in the explosion. But then Peterson's soul called to him, warning Thom that he must walk with the Lord or some crap. Thom missed most of it because he heard another voice emanating from Alpha, one he knew, one he wanted to hear. Thom focused on it, not believing it was really him. It couldn't be.

"Gregory?" Thom called to the distant voice. "Is that you?"

"Liar," Gregory yelled back to Thom. "You lied to me. You lied to yourself."

"But I meant it," Thom muttered as his heart sank. "I was going to meet you Berlin. But we died."

"Thom, you jackass," said the fading voice of Gregory. Then he said something else, something Thom couldn't make out at all.

As Alpha vanished into the distance, Thom stared on, numb.

Chapter 13
The Bleeding Afterlife

All around Thom, the newly freed souls rose into the sky while choirs gathered to welcome them in. The new souls rose to join choirs, formed new ones, or became individual souls. It seemed that very few faded if any at all. As Thom watched Alpha limp off, vanishing behind the gathering mist, guilt weighed on him, guilt over Gregory, guilt that went beyond not keeping his word to a friend. Thom felt it but somehow didn't understand it. He turned away from the long gone Alpha and went to find his father.

Thom's orb of red smoke hovered over to his estranged choir. They hovered low against the surface, projecting gold light down onto his father. They lifted away, revealing his father to be a murky green puddle pooled upon the animalsphere.

"We have kept him safe," said his choir.

Thom gathered his father from the surface, placing him around his equator, like he had with David. "Thank you so much for taking care of him," he told his choir.

"It was our honor," they said.

"That's quite a choir you got there," Snake said.

Thom kept his focus on feeding light to his dad and said, "I didn't gather it on purpose."

"I'm not talking about you," Snake said.

Thom looked up and gasped.

Also looking up, David muttered, "Mom, are you okay?"

"Of course, dear," said the large golden orb of Lida. "Are you okay?"

"Yeah, but all the souls around you…?"

Lida looked around herself. A vast number of souls had fallen into orbit around her and more kept coming.

"Oh," Lida said, "my friends are here."

"Your friends?" David asked. "Mom, what are you talking about?"

"I met them in the dark place. They're moms, like me. And just a lovely group of ladies. We're going to have a luncheon." Her voice dropped into a whisper as she added, "First, I'm planning a Meal of Condolence." Raising her voice again, she said, "Let me introduce you to everyone."

"But…" David muttered.

"Everyone, this is my boy, David."

"What a lovely boy you have," said Lida's growing choir of moms, all in unison. "Your mother has told us so much about you."

David asked, "How did she tell you anything?"

"We were having a lovely time in that dark place," his mom explained, "despite our impolite host."

"Your mother is truly a remarkable force of will," Prometheus said.

167

"Yeah," Thom mumbled as he hovered over to stand next to David.

Thom kept looking between the thin wisp of a ring that was his dad and the mighty golden sphere that was David's mom. He wanted to blame himself for his father's condition, to believe that he'd done something wrong while rescuing his dad. But Prometheus was right. It wasn't anything Thom had done that made a difference. Lida was the difference. Lida was a force of will. Thom couldn't have done any more for his dad.

"Your mother helped all of us," said her choir, the voices multiplying as they spoke. "We are so grateful for her kindness and friendship."

"Mom," David asked, "what…what…?"

"What 'what'?" Lida asked as she hovered closer to him, her gathering of souls moving with her.

Lida said, "You look thin, David. Have you been eating enough?"

"Um," David said, "I'm dead. So, I don't eat anymore."

"I suppose that's true," Lida said. "But you're looking thin. You should eat something."

"Again, mom, dead. Not alive. Not eating."

"Oh yes, dead." She drifted back a moment. "I'm dead. I keep forgetting that."

"It's understandable," Snake said. "You've been through a lot today."

"Yeah," Thom said, looking at the ring of vapor that was his father, "I'm surprised you're as together as you are." He reminded himself that his dad's condition wasn't his fault. Still, he couldn't shake the guilt.

"Oh no," Lida said. "If I'm dead that means that nice young man shot me. The poor boy."

David gasped, "You were shot?! And what do you mean 'poor boy'?"

"It wasn't the boy's fault," Lida said. "He was just a child. He shot me because his commander told him to, and his commander only told him to because...well...I punched his commander."

David shrank. "You punched...a soldier...a Nazi?"

"It was a reflex," she said. "The commander fellow punched your father. And before I knew it, there's my fist, knocking him to the floor. I swear, I didn't know I had it in me."

"Good for you," Snake said.

"Thank you, Snake."

"No, not *thank you*," David snapped. "You could've been killed!"

"She was killed," Snaked pointed out.

"How's your Aunt Milly?" she asked David, derailing his complaint.

"Uh...alive, I think."

"That's nice, dear. You sure you're not hungry? I'm about to make something."

"No," David said. "I'm still dead and still not hungry, thanks. And you really don't need to eat either, you know."

"Just because I'm dead doesn't mean it's time to stop living my life."

"Actually," Snake said, "that's kind of exactly what it means."

Her growing choir formed into slowly spinning arms like those of Buddha. They hovered low with Lida, eclipsing most of the sky over Thom. She was already larger than Nietzsche or the Druids, and she was rapidly catching up with the choir majestic of Buddha. As Thom looked on, more souls continued to join her.

"That's not normal," Thom asked, "is it?"

"Nope," Snake said, "very not normal."

"What the hell is going on?" David demanded of his mom.

"What do you mean?" Lida asked.

David grew two red fog tentacles so he could spread them wide at the spinning blue pinwheel around her gold orb. "That," David said. "I'm uncomfortable with *that*."

"Oh, they're a lovely group of ladies," Lida said. "You shouldn't be nervous. They're all happy to meet you."

"But there's so many of them."

"It's not so many."

"Yes, it is," Snake said.

"They're just some nice ladies I met while in that dark place. I was able to help them to compose themselves, after our rude host had us all flustered. Then while you had that door open for Corbin, our host was quite distracted. So, I opened another door and we walked out together. I'm glad to see you've been making friends too. You should go play with your friends. I promised the ladies a banquet once we got out. I fear it won't be a happy occasion, what with us all being deceased. But I'm hoping to help them move past it like I did."

"But…but…" David muttered, "I saved you and…I wanted…"

Lida paused. "What did you want, dear?"

"I…I wanted…" David's cloud churned with dark reds. Little sparks softly popped. "I wanted my mom," he muttered bitterly. "I didn't want to be sent away from my mom. Wh—why? I mean, I know why but…but…" His cloud rolled violently. The sparks popped louder.

Prometheus and Snake drifted back, away from the David-storm. Despite holding his father's haze, Thom moved closer, wanting to reach out to his troubled friend.

Lida said to her choir, "Do excuse me, please. I need a moment alone with my David."

"No need to apologize," they said together. "We understand."

The blue arms detached themselves from the gold orb that was Lida and floated up to a respectful distance from her conversation with her son. Though they didn't have her soul at their center, they continued orbiting around her absence.

"Well," Snake said, "that's another new one for me—first, Thom rejecting a choir—now the core of a choir stepping out for a moment. Amazing."

"Your species continues to surpass my estimates," Prometheus said.

Lida's giant orb descended to hover above her son. Sparks continued to pop off David. Thom stood close. He wasn't sure why David remained angry after saving his mom. It seemed David didn't either.

"We clearly need to talk," Lida said and grew a small tentacle that reached out for him.

David backed away, almost into Thom. "If you touch me, we'll go into a memory, but I don't think you'll like the memory we'll end up in."

"Oh, David," she said, "I know where we're going. Now, come to your mother."

David hovered closer to the arm that seemed far too small for her massive orb. He too grew an arm and reached for Lida.

"Are you sure you want to do that?" Thom warned as he instinctively moved to stop David. Not thinking, Thom touched David as David touched Lida. They all fell into a memory together, even Thom's dad.

Thom found himself kneeling over his father. They each wore their respective uniforms. His father was unconscious while Thom pressed a bandage to his shoulder. He'd done this for other men in battle, keeping pressure on a wound to stop the bleeding. But there was no blood. Instead, under the bandage he saw a soft glowing light.

Looking up, Thom found that they'd returned to the memory of Lida sending David away—or rather the memory of the pier where it happened. There wasn't a crowd this time, no commotion, no clamor. Just empty cement framed by big black bows of ocean liners. It was dark, no sun, no stars or moon. Shadows shrouded all but the great metal hulls.

And in the middle of the concrete pier, David stood, dressed in his gear from D-Day, helmet, grenades, everything. His hands clenched his rifle, while his jaw clenched his teeth. Before him, his mother wore the blue dress with the lace collar, the one she'd worn the day she sent David away.

She walked forward and reached out for his face, but she pulled back before touching him. "You look handsome in your uniform," she said, her smile shallow, unable to veil the tears behind it. "I wish I'd gotten to see you in it while I was alive."

"So do I," David said through his teeth. "I tried."

"What do you mean? Tried what, dear?"

"I was going to look for you after we won the war."

"Look for me?" she asked, her shrouding smile becoming sincere. "Across the entire continent?"

"I wanted to save you," David said, now staring at his boots, still coated in the sands of Pointe du Hoc. "I had it in my head that I'd fight my way to Berlin," he said, "and then, once the Nazis were done for, I'd desert and go look for you. It was a dumb idea. I was an idiot."

"You were my brave boy," Lida said, her tears painting lines down her cheeks. "You always were brave. Especially this day." She gestured at the setting around them.

As her gesture passed over him, Thom felt like an intruder for being part of this moment. He considered pulling his mind out, taking his father with him. But Lida cast a warm smile in Thom's direction, telling him not to worry about it. Thom still considered leaving but decided David might need a friend after this, or during.

"You were just a little boy," Lida continued, her smile turning to her son, "but you did exactly what I asked you to do. You called your Aunt Milly mom and everything. She sent a letter back to me through one of the maids on your ship. Milly wrote it just before you arrived in the Americas. That nice young woman, the one who worked on your boat, she risked her life to bring me that letter, to tell me that my baby boy was safe. She was a good woman and you, David, you were a good, brave boy. I could not have been prouder."

"But," David said, his gun suddenly gone, freeing his hands to ball into trembling fists. "But…but, I'm so angry at you."

"I know you are," she said softly, "and you should be."

With his eyes still fixed on his sandy boots, he yelled, "No, I shouldn't!"

His words sent a bolt of scarlet lightning firing out of the top of his steel helmet and into the blackness above. Thom covered his dad with his body, as if protecting him from debris kicked up by an artillery strike.

"I can't stop myself from being angry," David growled, as the buzzing red bolt subsided. "I can't stop being mad at you. I know I shouldn't be. I know you did the right thing. I know you would've gotten out too if you could've. But I'm still angry. I should be angry at the Nazis and I am. And I'm angry at the world for being horrible. But…but I'm so angry at you. You sent me away!"

Another bolt of dark red fired upwards. Rolling thunder followed. Thom again shielded his dad as if this were a battlefield instead of a memory.

As the sound subsided, Lida took a long, firm breath. Then she looked David straight in the eye and said, "I'll tell you the same thing I told your father after I came home without you. You absolutely should be angry. It was a horrible thing that I did to you, sending you away like that. But it was also the right thing. There were no good options, so I picked the one that would keep you alive. I did the right thing and it's perfectly fine for you to be angry at me."

She stared straight into David's eyes, her gaze unwavering. Even from across the pier, Thom could see her barely holding back tears.

David's face bubbled with competing emotions until he screamed, "Fuck you!" He fell to his knees, releasing bolts of lightning like cannon fire, scorching the sides of the ships, filling the small dark space with thunder. "Fuck you!" he yelled again as hot tears dripped into his lap. Grinding the heels of his hands into his eyes, he whimpered, "Fuck you, fuck you, fuck you..."

As his cursing devolved into sobs and the thunder dimmed into silence, his mom said, "There, there, David, let it out. But with less profanity if you can, please. I know it hurts, but there's no need for that language."

"I'm sorry," he moaned softly. "I didn't mean to...I didn't mean any of it."

"You did mean it, and you didn't mean it at the same time," Lida said, "just like your father. You're headstrong, just like him too, but you have my heart. I'm sorry I wasn't there for you. I'm sorry the world was what it was. But one thing I am not sorry about is that I brought my baby boy into the world. I could not be prouder of the man you became. Except for the cursing."

Laughter broke through David's tears, shoulder-shrugging laughter mixed with heaving, choking sobs.

"Okay," Lida said, her hand reaching out. "Enough crying. People are waiting and we shouldn't leave them to worry about us. And we dragged your friend Thom into this with us. Hello, Thom! I'm sure he wants to get back too."

David took her hand, and she helped him off the floor. They hugged.

As they let go, David said, "I love you, Mom."

"I love you, too," Lida said. Then she put her fists firmly on her hips and added, "But I'll tell you one thing, young man, I better not hear that language out of you again. I don't care how they talk in that Americas Army you joined, I raised you better than that and I don't want to hear that kind of language out of you again."

David nodded solemnly. "Yes, Mom. I'm sorry, Mom."

She then hugged her son again. He hugged her back, his tears quietly flowing. Once that had subsided, Lida gently pulled them all out of the memory. When their consciousness arrived back in their souls, choirs filled the sky, including Lida's blue pinwheel arms, which nearly eclipsed Buddha. Thom found his dad still a thin ring of mist, but thicker than before the memory. David's cloud was no longer red, nor was it a cloud. David had become a silver sphere like Prometheus or Snake.

Thom gawked at the transformation. Why hadn't he found nirvana like David clearly had? Thom still didn't get the idea of nirvana, but he knew it when he saw it. And when he looked at himself, he saw the red of confused anger still raging within him,

176

anger he couldn't explain. And his father was so far from nirvana that he barely maintained his existence. Then there was Lida who was still gold but clearly close to nirvana, so close that she'd attracted a massive choir. If Thom could pull himself together, it would help him help his dad, he was sure. What was holding Thom back? He had no idea.

Lida said to David, "You look much better. I'm glad we talked. But you do need to eat more."

"But, Mom…"

"I saw what you looked like in that memory," she said as she ascended toward her choir. "I'll be back later—and you're going to eat something—but I have grown-up things to attend to right now. You go play with your friends. Oh, and Thom, thank you again for looking after my boy. And it was so nice meeting all of you."

Snake waved a silver tentacle at her and said, "Bye, Mrs. David's Mom."

"Call me Lida," she said, still floating up.

"But, Mom…"

"I love you, David, but I do have to go now," she sang down to him as she rejoined her choir. "I'll see you soon."

"But…I love you, too, Mom."

As Lida's gold orb rejoined her blue choir, a flash sent an image into everyone's heads, an image of what the collection of souls was experiencing in there. Lida's choir was nothing but moms, moms from around the world and throughout time, thousands or perhaps millions of them. And David's mom seemed to know each of them personally.

As promised, they were at a feast. It was in a nice but modest meeting room, but it seemed to stretch off forever in all directions. Cement pillars held up a plain ceiling over an endless sea of tables, each adorned with daisies, baskets of bread and rolls, plates of deviled and hardboiled eggs, bowls of cooked and raw vegetables and lentils, and coffee, tea, and lots of red and white wine for as far as the eye could see. The moms gathered to eat and drink and give comfort to each other for their losses. Somehow, Lida sat at every table.

Sensing Thom and the others looking on, the moms looked up and said as one, "This is grown up time, you boys go play."

Together, Thom and the others came out of the vision.

"Wow," Snake said, "your mom is a real people person. What was all that?"

"I think that was the Meal of Condolences," David said, "it's a tradition when someone dies."

"Yeah, well, makes sense," Snake said. "A lot of dead people around here."

As her massive choir drifted up and away, Lida's golden orb turned silver. In a flash, the color rolled down each arm of her pinwheel. She was now a slowly spinning storm of pure silver. She'd reached nirvana, and she'd taken her entire choir with her. Meanwhile, Thom remained a red blob of fog barely keeping his father alive. He wondered if he would ever stop failing his family.

As Thom stared on in silence, David asked, "What just happened?"

"She has become a choir majestic," Prometheus said. "Like Buddha but much sooner…far too soon."

"Yeah," Snake said, "I can't believe she gathered so many moms so fast."

"It's her thing," David said, still watching her drift off. "She's always been a planner. She organized all kinds of stuff, even stuff people didn't celebrate until she came along. She'd organize luncheons and banquets for anything—like every time someone needed a Meal of Condolences, or when my father performed a bris, or when there was a bar mitzvah, or a break-fast after Yom Kippur, or for Passover, or Hanukah, and weddings, even birthdays…so yeah, I guess that was her thing."

Snake said, "So, what are we going to call her when she becomes a soul well?"

Prometheus replied, "The end of days."

"Omega, then," Snake said. "She shall be the soul well Omega, the soul well to end all soul wells…on this planet anyway."

From above, Buddha boomed, "Lida has found a balance within herself that she is sharing with the moms. I sense no greed within her. She will never form a soul well."

"You sense no greed *now*," Snake pointed out. "Things can change."

"Mom," David called up to her, "I don't want you to become a soul well."

"A soul well?" she asked. "You mean one of those dark places, like the one I was in? Oh my, I would never. That would be rude. But I'm afraid I really must go now. Bye, everyone." Then she hurried off toward the horizon with her choir majestic, while Thom and the others stared on.

***

As the choir majestic of Lida drifted over the horizon, other newly freed souls gathered around Thom and David. The gathering quickly devolved into a chattering swarm of multi-colored clouds, all asking Thom and David for different things, but also the same thing.

"My mom is in there like yours."

"My dad, can you show me how to get him out?"

"I think my sister was in that other dark place."

"My brother."

"My wife."

"My husband."

"My best friend."

"My baby boy."

"My little girl."

"How did you do it?"

"How can we do what you did?"

The many-hued multitude pressed in from all sides, choirs and free souls alike. Even translucent puddles of mist came crawling. Despite the gathering of souls clamoring for help, Thom tried to focus on feeding light into the ring of haze that was his father. Why did David's mom do so well while Thom could barely keep his father from fading? What had Thom done wrong?

As these thoughts rattled through his mind, over the chattering mob, Thom's dad whispered to him, "It's all my fault."

"What is?" Thom asked. "I don't understand."

"I'll show you." His dad's ring reached in and touched him. Thom fell into another memory and became his dad, standing on a porch, watching his own father, Thom's grandfather, getting into a Model T. It was packed with men, all in uniform, all heading to Mexico, leaving the little boy that was Thom's dad standing on the porch, alone without a father again.

Then Thom was his dad a couple years later, opening a letter from his wayward father; the letter was full of frustration at the pointlessness of chasing Mexican bandits that they could never find.

Then Thom was his dad dressed in his uniform, about to leave for the war in Europe, the first war, and just as Thom's grandfather was finally coming back from Mexico and all the other places the Army had sent him.

Thom braced himself, expecting the memory of Flanders Fields to come next. But instead, they went backwards in time; Thom was his dad as a teen, sitting on a log. Another boy sat beside him, the boy with the freckles who Thom had seen in past visions from his father. They gazed across a lush valley stretching off to the horizon. The other boy put his arm around Thom and laid his head on Thom's shoulder. Thom felt his body heat rise, his pulse quickened.

With a jolt, Thom snapped out of his father's memory. Disoriented, he found himself back in his cloud body, still surrounded by the multi-colored mob of souls and choirs baying for help. Looking down, Thom found that his dad's soul had grown in mass, extending out in a dense disk of dark blue.

"Dad?" Thom asked. "Can you hear me? Can you talk?"

His father's haze shuddered and said, "I'm so sorry."

"About what?" Thom begged.

"About attacking the soul wells," Snake said.

Looking up from his father's soul, Thom found that Snake and Prometheus had joined him and David at the center of the mob.

David's solid silver soul shimmered with brilliance as he announced, "We will help you, Thom and me. We will help all of you."

"Well," Snake said, "Thom will help you, mostly."

"What?" Thom snapped.

"They believe that you're the key to saving their loved ones," Prometheus explained.

"Yup," Snake said, "it's that messiah thing again."

"But…but…" Thom stuttered. "What about David?"

"My mom freed herself," David said. "And she saved me. I saved no one. And after what happened to Corbin…" David trailed off, his silver shell momentarily dimming.

"And you saved your dad," Snake said.

Prometheus said, "You are the only one who has battled a soul well and won. You may be the key to defeating them."

"No," Thom said. "I'm just a guy who wanted to save my dad. And I'm not sure if I really saved him. I mean, look at him. He's barely alive. And then there's what happened to Corbin."

"Corbin wasn't you," David said. "That was me. I was the one who lost Corbin. You got your dad out. My mom got herself out. And I fucked up. We need you, Thom."

"No," Thom said, his red gaseous sphere contracting, "you need David or Prometheus or maybe Lida, not me. With my dad like this…I don't know. It's not me. I'm not the one you need. I can't."

"You have to," said his dad's faint voice. "This is what you were born for."

"Dad? Are you okay?"

"I will be," his dad said, his cloud ring gathering a little more mass. "But don't worry about me. You have to worry about these people and their families. And our family. You saved me and now you're going to save us all."

Then his dad reached in with a nub of fog and touched Thom again, pulling him back into that memory of his father's front porch. Though Thom's dad had been a little boy at the time, his dad now appeared as an adult, dressed as he had been for his ill-fated run across Flanders Fields. Thom stood beside him, wearing his uniform from D-Day.

The porch they stood upon was part of a house that was sur-rounded by nothing, across a dirt road from nothing, and with more nothing stretching off into the empty distance, a nothing only interrupted by the dust billowing behind a Model T as it drove off into eternity.

His dad placed a hand on Thom's shoulder. "That's your pops," he said. "I'm the last 'Jeff' and you're the last 'Thom' but none of that is your fault and none of it is important right now."

"How is it not my fault?" Thom pleaded. "I failed in what I was born to do."

His dad gripped Thom's shoulder tight and said, "*This*, the help everyone is asking you for, this is what you were born for. I can't say I saw it coming, of course, but this is it. This is what the line of Stoneshield has been leading to, stopping those monsters from destroying all of us. You have to help everyone. You are the one to organize and lead them."

As Thom stared into his father's steady gaze, he thought about what he'd gone through to free his dad, the memories he had to fight and the physical battle between clouds. It was true, he had defeated a soul well. But not completely, and he hadn't done it alone.

Thom looked past his dad, to that rising plume of dust from the car as his grandfather drove off to a war that was not a war. That non-war was pointless, but the struggle facing Thom now was the most important conflict in human history.

"You're right," he said, "I need to organize them into an army, and I need to do it now before the soul wells get even stronger. But we're not done with this conversation. You're going to explain what you mean by it's all your fault."

Though he yearned for answers, Thom pulled them out of the memory, for now.

Chapter 14
Behind the Grey Veil

Thom sent the larger choirs to circle the afterlife and alert those not already aware that there would be a war council. This would affect every soul in the afterlife, so Thom felt they all should have a chance to speak their minds and to join the effort if they chose. While Buddha, Nietzsche, and other choirs fanned out to spread the word, the newly dead of Europe and North America drifted toward the impending meeting over the North Atlantic. They approached in a steady march of murky hues, clouds, and puddles, gradually congregating around David, Prometheus, Snake, Thom, and his dad. As they gathered, some formed or joined choirs, but many remained independent souls.

As the clouds gathered around them, David asked, "Is it just me or are there a lot more free souls than before?"

"There are indeed," Prometheus said. "I've never seen so many independent souls at once."

From around Thom, his dad said, "They're all young. What happened to all the people from my day?"

Thom took a moment, surprised his dad was talking instead of muttering a vague apology. "Uh, I think most have faded, or they're still in the soul wells."

Prometheus said, "They marched in willingly."

Thom said, "I think my generation is still going in willingly, too."

Snake said, "But the younger ones are making it up here in larger numbers."

"I wonder why," Prometheus said.

"I think they're not buying the line from the soul wells anymore," David said. For Thom's dad, he added, "The soul wells use our religions to dupe us into thinking that they're gods or heaven or whatever. I'm guessing it just ain't working like it used to. Maybe the damage we did helped the living. Maybe the living are just getting smarter."

Thom's dad said, "You know, I'm not sure how I ended up in that thing. I don't even know if I went in willingly or not. I don't remember."

"I'm not surprised," Snake said. "That monster did a real number on you."

"How are you feeling?" Thom asked his dad, still surprised at how clearheaded he seemed.

"Alive…kind of. I think I can stand on my own. Let me try." Without help from anyone, Thom's dad gathered himself into a small blue orb of fog.

Thom was again surprised. He gazed around at the gathering meeting. They had a little time before all the souls would get there. So, Thom told the others to greet the new arrivals, while he and his father drifted off to finish their conversation.

His father's dark blue fog ball hovered close to the ground, but he no longer needed Thom to keep him from fading. Thom's cloud was thick and spherical, but it was still gas, not solid like Prometheus, Snake, and now David. Together Thom and his dad moved from the epicenter of the meeting, out to where the paths of the approaching souls spread out, like spokes on a wheel, offering Thom and his dad some small amount privacy.

Thom stopped and looked back at the gathering. At its base, the thinnest of the free souls pooled upon the golden surface while thicker clouds hovered over them, and thicker still hovered above those. And over the free souls hung the smallest choirs, mere fog-banks dwarfed by the more robust clouds above them, clouds that were then dwarfed by the great spinning pinwheels that hovered higher still. But even the greatest of the pinwheels appeared small as they huddled together beneath the choirs majestic of David's mom and Buddha. Together they looked like a mountain of fog painted in primary colors, surrounded by a sea of shimmering gold.

With few souls passing near them, Thom turned to his dad, ready to demand to know why his dad kept apologizing to him. But there was something else that baffed Thom, something he needed to know. So, he asked, "Why did I keep seeing that short guy in your memory?"

"Short guy?"

"Short, skinny, wearing a business suit and a fedora," Thom said, "constantly smoking a cigar, at least every time I saw him."

As Thom explained, his dad started chuckling. "I know who you're talking about."

"Then who is it?"

"Thom, I have to explain something first…a big something."

"What?" Thom demanded, his red smog growing bright. "Who's the guy? What's with that kid in that other memory of you—the memory where you were sitting on a log with him. And what do you have to apologize for? I'm the one who didn't have any kids. I didn't even get married. Me. I failed, not you."

His dad's blue cloud shrank beneath Thom's burning red. "Thom, haven't you ever wondered why you never got married?"

Thom said, "I know why. It's because I was immature. I wanted to play in the woods. I wanted to pretend that I was in the Scouts."

"No, Thom, you didn't get married because you were like me."

"But you got married. I don't get it."

"I know you don't," his dad said. "I think I need to show you." He floated closer and touched Thom, pulling them both into a memory.

As the sun rose behind the thinning fall foliage, Thom found himself standing beside a canvas tent. Two pair of feet bulged in the end of a single sleeping bag protruding through the tent flaps. Someone touched Thom's shoulder and he turned to find himself face to face with his father. They both wore their uniforms again, but no gear or helmets. Behind his dad, silhouetted by the sunrise, was that log.

Thom said, "That's where that boy was with you, sitting ...and he…"

"He put his head on my shoulder," his dad said.

Thom's heart raced. He didn't belong here, at this campsite, in this memory, or anywhere near any of this. His feet wanted to run, and he wanted to let them. But he needed to know, so he kept them planted and reluctantly asked, "Is that the guy in the suit?"

His dad chuckled. "No. This guy is Brian. I knew him back in high school."

"So…what's going on? Why are we here?"

Gesturing toward the feet mingling in the sleeping bag, his dad said, "This is what I was talking about, Thom. This is why I'm sorry that I wasn't there for you. I could've helped you understand this part of who you are. It's my fault for not being there."

Thom took an involuntary step back. "What are you talking about?"

"You know what I'm talking about."

"No," Thom said, "I really don't."

His dad snorted grimly. "Wow, the world really did a number on you. I am so sorry. It's not easy being like us."

"Like us how?" Thom demanded, his pulse pounding in his ears.

His dad looked him square in the eye and said, "A poof."

Thom took another step back. "A what?"

"A poof," his dad repeated. "A nance. A fruit. A blue discharge. A boy who likes boys."

"What do you mean?" Thom said, almost panting. "You mean you?"

"No, *us*."

"Me?"

"Yes," his dad said, "the both of us. I've seen it in you, in your memories. You and that Gil kid when you were younger. And then there was Sergeant Holt."

"Gregory?" Thom said. "He's like a brother to me. And you, you and mom...and me, you had me...so...how?"

"Ah," his dad said, almost singing it. "Your mother, she understood me. In a way, she was like me, like we were meant to be together."

Smelling the thick scent of cigar smoke, Thom turned to find the short, slight fellow in the business suit and fedora, the cigar smoke curling in front of his face. Only this time his face wasn't in shadow. The campsite memory's morning light shown upon it, cutting through the grey, winding smoke to illuminate the narrow jaw line, the high cheek bones, the curling lashes, the thick lips, and the bright blue eyes that belonged to Thom's mother, dressed as a man.

Thom screamed.

***

The memory around Thom shattered and fell away, leaving him and his father back in their cloud selves resting upon the ocean of animal souls. Thom's red shell pulsed light while his sphere rapidly contracted and expanded. His dad's blue fog hovered above the surface, more stable and a little larger than before the memory. Around them, the thin stream of free souls and small choirs continued their pilgrimage to the gathering of souls not far away.

"What was that?" Thom gasped.

"Your mother," his dad said, "dressed like a man. She was small, like you said, but, wow, her shoulders sure filled out a suit, didn't they?"

"Dad!"

"Sorry. She's your mom. I forgot myself for a second there. But, like I said, she understood me. And I understood her. Like we were made for each other. But the world wasn't okay with either of us being ourselves. Hell, we had to go to an out-of-town tailor for that suit. We fed him a story about it being for an elaborate inside joke...I don't even remember it all, but I don't think he believed us. He just wanted our money, and then he wanted us the hell out of his shop. Him and the whole rest of the world wanted to pretend we didn't exist."

"Okay," Thom said, while his soul churned, "so you like boys and mom...?"

"Your mom was a boy, kind of. But she liked boys, like I like boys, and you like boys."

"But I didn't like boys. I never liked boys."

"Yes, you did, and you still do," his dad said, his blue soul slowly growing larger. "But I'm not surprised that you didn't know. You were such a good kid that when the world told you to like girls, not boys, you did...well, mostly. You never had someone like Brian, someone who helped you understand. And you never had a woman like your mother. Fortunately for me, we found each other somehow. And then we had you."

"See," Thom said, "you loved Mom. You can't be a poof."

"It's called being bisexual," said someone.

191

Thom turned to find that a choir of two had paused behind him on their way to the meeting. One side was bright red, the other was dark red. Each was a half-sphere that came together to form a single hazy orb. "Your dad was bisexual," continued the dark red half. "Deal with it."

"Please forgive Andrea," the bright half said. "She's still...she's angry. Don't let her direct it at you. I'm Sara, by the way."

"I'm Jeff," Thom's dad said. "And this is my son, Thom."

"Nice to meet you," said the Sara half. "And sorry for intruding but, yes, that's called being a bisexual."

Thom contracted. "Being a what?"

"You've never heard the word 'bisexual'?" asked the Andrea half.

"How long ago did you die?" Sara asked.

"D-Day."

"Oh, well," Sara said, "no wonder. I'm not sure the word existed back then."

"When did you die?" Thom's dad asked.

"Stupid gas leak," Andrea grumbled. "Stupid oven. Knew we shouldn't have let your brother install it."

"Right after ringing in 2020," Sara said.

"2020?" his dad asked.

"2019 becoming the year 2020," Sara said.

Thom's dad mumbled, "It's been that long?"

"But...?" Thom said. "You said my dad...?"

"That he's bisexual," Andrea finished for him.

Sara explained, "Bisexual means, that you like both sexes...both men and women...you know, biblically. Personally,

I believe everyone is bisexual with a preference, going one way or the other."

"Not me," Andrea said.

"And society pushes us one way or the other," Sara continued, "thus creating the illusion of gay and straight."

"It was her master's thesis in sociology," Andrea griped. "It was a good paper, but I'm not bisexual at all. I only like girls. Sorry to disprove your paper, babe."

Above them, a great blue cloud paused. As it spoke, Thom knew it to be the choir of Socrates. And it still felt weird having information shoved into his head like that. The collective voice of the choir of Socrates said, "Some people prefer snails and others prefer oysters. But if one seasons a snail to taste like an oyster…"

"Then you get my Beatrice," Thom's dad said. "And she sure was handsome in that suit."

"I get it," Thom said before his dad could say any more. "You had a thing for men and you and mom…did a thing. But I'm no nance. I just never found the right girl."

"You never tried to find the right girl," his dad said.

Socrates said, "It sounds as if there is no *right girl* for Thom."

"Unless she was the right kind of girl," Sara said.

"No," Andrea said, "he's gay like me. I'm gay and only gay."

"But I'm not gay," Thom said.

"You poor, mixed up boy," said another choir, now pausing above Thom. It was a bright pink billowing mass—a color of choir Thom had not seen before. "Let us help you find your way," said the pink choir.

They beckoned him in, and when Thom gazed into the shared thoughts of the choir, he saw something he'd only ever heard about. People in little or no clothing, lounging on sofas or on piles of pillows, surrounded by walls of marble, sandstone, or cheap wood paneling. And those not lounging did something else, something together; he saw them, men and women lying together, biblically, with both men and women.

Thom lurched out of the image. "Holy shit," he yelled. "What the...what the...?"

Andrea looked inside the pink choir's reality and came out chuckling. "Looks like I found the party."

Sara ignored her and turned her attention to Thom. "You okay?"

"What the hell was that?"

"Fun," Andrea answered before Sara could.

"Can you stop being a pig for a minute," Sara said. "The poor man can't even handle his own sexuality. He's not ready for...for...all that. Let's focus on the fact that Thom is mostly gay."

"He sounds all gay to me," Andrea said.

"I'm not gay," Thom said. "I'm not happy about any of this."

Andrea and Sara broke out laughing.

"Gay means homosexual now," Sara said. "It means you're a boy who likes boys."

"I'm not that either."

From above, the pink choir said, "You come from a time of many sexual issues, Thom."

"I don't like boys," Thom insisted again.

"You liked one boy," his dad said. "Well, two boys really, but the boy you really liked was that Sergeant Holt. Look inside yourself. You'll find the truth. Hell, I found it in you without looking for it. If you want, I can help you find it too."

His dad extended an arm of blue fog toward him. Thom cringed from it at first but then he stopped and let his father take him into another memory, hoping he'd be able to help his dad understand that Thom was not a blue discharge.

But where they ended up wasn't the memory Thom expected.

***

The first thing Thom noticed was the smell, thick and musky and somewhat putrid, but also alluring. He again wore his D-Day uniform, and his dad wore his uniform standing beside Thom on the wooden floor, at the end of the long bench, framed on both sides by lockers, short ones, like the ones for kids barely in their teens.

Recognizing this place, Thom cringed. He wanted to get out of there and run far, far away, but he didn't understand why. "Why are we here?" he demanded.

"Because this is where it happened," his dad said.

"Nothing happened here. Not ever." Thom turned away, but it didn't work. The scene turned with him, keeping those benches and small lockers in front of him.

"I saw it in your memories, Thom." His father spoke soft and slow. "I saw it in this moment, even if you pretended not to."

Thom snapped, "What moment?"

Then he appeared, Chuck, the biggest kid in the seventh grade...and the hairiest. He stood there in his underwear with his bushy black eyebrows pushed together like a pair of fierce caterpillars locked in battle. His lips tight, fists clenched. His chest broad and arms thick. And those hairy legs. Though in the real memory this place was packed with kids getting changed, this version held only Chuck, frozen in time.

Thom knew this moment. He'd tried to forget it, tried hard, but it kept resurfacing, and Thom kept shoving it back into the darkest corners of his mind. But nothing had happened here. They just looked at each other and then nothing. Nothing happened. So why did Thom keep thinking about this, even years later? Why was he here now?

Touching Thom's shoulder, his dad said, "You honestly don't know, do you? I mean, you do but you don't, do you?"

"Know what?" Thom demanded, unable to stop looking at Chuck, who seemed older than he had been at the time. This looked like an adult version of the Chuck, a mature Chuck, a taller Chuck, a Chuck with his inevitable muscles filled in.

Thom's dad said, "This was the moment when *it* turned on and you turned *it* off. And you did a real good job of keeping it turned off after that."

Gazing at the still frame of Chuck, now a young man in his twenties, an idealized version of what Chuck could've but probably didn't grow into, a strong Chuck with thick legs and arms and a barrel of a chest. But that look stayed on his face. His curled lip and wrinkled nose, his slight backward lean, all etched into Thom's mind forever.

196

"Earlier that day," his dad said, "the other kids had been making fun of one of the boys, calling him a poof. And then you came in here and this happened."

"I didn't even know what a poof was," Thom said, his voice low. "I found out while they were picking on that kid. They said he threw like a poof and then…"

"They said a lot of other stuff," his dad said as he placed a hand on Thom's shoulder. "Saying things about what the poofs like to do with each other. And this kid had been one of the loudest, yelling about the fruits buggering each other."

"Yeah," Thom said, taking a step closer to the adult version of Chuck. "And then we came in here to get changed and…"

"And you looked at him," his dad finished for Thom. "You looked at him the way other boys look at girls."

"Yeah," Thom whispered. It was the first time he'd ever admitted that to anyone, even to himself. The urge to run away from it all surged through him, but he couldn't even look away. He stood there staring at Chuck like other boys stared at girls.

"Then what happened?" his dad asked.

"He looked back," Thom said. "Like that…with that look on his face. Like he was going to puke or punch me or both."

"And you froze." His dad squeezed Thom's shoulder.

"Then something happened," Thom said, finally ripping his eyes away with much relief. "Someone knocked into someone else and started shoving, and Chuck punched someone. But it wasn't serious. Just goofing."

"But you got dressed and got out of there. And you turned it off."

Tears filled Thom's eyes. He didn't know why. "I did. I just stopped thinking about it. Or I tried to." As his dad squeezed his shoulder tighter, the tears rolled down Thom's face. "I tried, I really tried."

"I know you did," his dad said, tears now pouring down his face as well. "Folks told you boys like girls and only girls. And you had our family name hung around your neck like a stone. It wasn't fair to you. None of it."

Thom fell against his dad, gushing tears into his government-issue coat. "I wanted to like girls. I swear I did."

"I know," he said, hugging Thom. "But you shouldn't've had to. And I shouldn't've left you. I'm so sorry."

Thom said, "You had to go. It was war."

"I didn't have to." He released Thom and hung his head. "I wasn't called up. I

volunteered. It was stupid. That whole war was stupid."

Thom found himself in Flanders Fields again, with the trenches and the machine gun nest but no soldiers. The ground beneath their feet was mud but they didn't sink into it.

"It was your Pops," his dad said through a grimace. "I got a letter telling me he was coming home from the Army. I'd been waiting for him my whole damn life and now that I was all grown up and living my life without him ever being around, he just says he's finally coming home for good. The jerk left me without a dad and thinks he's gonna waltz in and…and then I did the most boneheaded thing I ever done. I asked to go to Europe. This place," he said as he waved his arms around in disgust. "I came to this stupid place so a bunch of dumb fucking generals could tell us to go walk on fucking water."

"You volunteered so you could…what? Get back at Pops?"

"I didn't want to see him. I got all steamed up just thinking about him, and I…I was a simpleton. I didn't know what I was signing up for…and then I did to you what he did to me. I left you without a dad." As the tears again streamed down his face, his dad said, "I'm so sorry, Thom."

Also welling up, Thom pulled him into a hug. "It's okay, Dad. You didn't know. You couldn't know how bad it was."

"It was stupid," he whimpered, "just stupid. I should've been there for you…so stupid."

As they held each other, the tears flowing from both of them, the vision of Flanders Fields melted like watercolors in the rain. When they came out of the memory, Thom found his father's fog had grown denser and taken on a brighter shade of blue, as well. Around them hovered the billowing blue cloud of Socrates, the dyad of Sara and Andrea, and the pink choir of upsetting images.

"That's what I'm so sorry about," his dad said. "I left such a burden on you. And because I was a bonehead, trying to get back at my dad. I should've been there to help you learn who you were. Like Brian helped me."

A thousand little moments flashed through Thom's mind, all with Gregory, all meaningless, at least at the time they seemed meaningless—a look, a brush of the hand, a subtle joke that could've meant something else and probably did…definitely did. But he understood now, he understood it all. Thom felt sick to his stomach.

"Oh my god," he muttered, "I've been such an ass."

"About which part?" Andrea asked. "Not knowing you're gay or not knowing that your dad was gay?"

"Be nice," Sara said.

"I was just asking a question."

"Gregory," Thom said. "I was so blind. And he knew the whole time."

"It's okay," his dad said. "You didn't know."

Thom stammered, "But why didn't he...how come he didn't...?"

"You were both career military," his dad said. "He knew better. And you..."

Andrea cut in. "Greg probably didn't know who you were, not really. I mean, you clearly didn't know who you were, so how could he? Maybe you'd freak out and get him kicked out of the Army."

"Or at least stop being his friend," Sara added.

"How could I be so dumb?" Thom asked himself.

"That's life," Andrea said. "You do a bunch of dumb shit you regret and then you die."

"Can you stop about the oven already," Sara said.

"I'm not talking about the fucking oven that your dumbass brother killed us with."

"Yes, you fucking are, and you need to get over it."

"I can't get over it," Andrea said, "because I'm fucking dead."

Andrea glowed red. Sara glowed red back.

"Fine," Andrea said, "I was talking about your asshole brother and the gas lines he didn't seal right...but I was talking about other stuff, too. Like that's the only stupid thing that happened to me."

"Do you two mind?" Thom's dad said. "I was talking to my son here."

The choir of Socrates drifted closer and said, "You seem distant, Thom, but not in a memory. Are you with us?"

Thom said, "Yeah, I'm here but Gregory's not. He's still in there."

"I know," his dad said, "but that's not your fault either."

"I don't care who's fault it is," Thom said. "I need to make things right between me and him. I need to make things right for everyone. I'm going to get him out of that well. I'm going to get everyone out. Let's join the others. It's time to start this meeting."

Chapter 15
War Council of Purgatory

With the choir of Socrates, the pink choir, and the dyad of Sara and Andrea following them, Thom and his dad drifted toward the gathering place where many choirs and free souls had already come together. The fog of individual souls formed a wide ring upon the golden surface of the animalsphere. Small choirs hovered above the individuals, larger choirs hovered above the small, and larger still above them. They stacked choir upon choir up to the top where the choirs majestic of Buddha and Lida hovered above them all. Together, the souls and choirs looked like a great tower of multi-colored fog.

Though he knew that the fate of all sentient life everywhere and throughout time could rest upon what they did now, Thom couldn't stop thinking about Gregory. How could Thom have been so blind to himself and to the man he loved? His dad lived through the same social pressure as Thom, but he figured himself out. And his grandfather…was his grandfather a poof, even a little? Thom realized that, even though he lived with his grandfather until Thom was six, he didn't really know the man at all. He remembered him as a stern pile of leathery wrinkles who sat in *his* chair and read the papers and listened to the radio and rarely spoke in more than a grunt.

Drifting ahead of the choirs that followed them, Thom asked his dad, "Was Pops like this too? Like us?"

"If he was," his dad said, "I never saw it. But honestly, I barely met the man. He could've been a poof; he could've been the Tsar for all I knew. I had an uncle who spent more time being my father than he did. Dad was in the army before I was born. I only heard war stories from Uncle Marv."

"Great Uncle Marv?" Thom said. "That's where I heard war stories about you, and the whole family all the way back to the Battle of Dunbar. Is that crest thing really real?"

"You mean, the one with the chip off that rock in it?"

Uncle Marv claimed he had *the* coat of arms brought to America by their family when the U.S. was still a British colony. If true, it held a chip off the rock that their ancestor had used to shelter a fallen knight during the Battle of Dunbar, a memento of the moment that started their family legacy.

"Yeah, is that chip really off that rock?" Thom asked.

"I don't know," his dad said. "Could be real, could be baloney. But I know the Army should've paid Marv as a recruiter. I wonder if Uncle Marv had a hand in my dad going off forever. The Army was my dad's whole life. Me and my mom definitely weren't. We hardly saw him, so he could've been a poof, who knows. Brian, my boyfriend back in school, he was the one who understood who I really was. He helped me through. We were on a wrestling team together and… it was obvious, to him at least."

"I wish I'd understood," Thom said, his smoggy red sphere contracting. "I wasted my whole life, wasted Gregory's life too."

His dad extended a tentacle of blue fog to wrap around Thom. To Thom's surprise, it didn't trigger a memory. "That's in the past now," his dad said. "You need to focus on what's next. You might still have a future with Gregory."

"Thanks, Dad," Thom said. "Thank you for being here for me."

"I'm glad I finally got to be here for you like I always should've been."

As they neared the meeting, the tower of souls and choirs seemed to grow until Thom found himself staring up from its base. It appeared a vast undulating storm painted in all the primary colors. While Socrates and the pink choir rose to join the upper layers, Thom, his dad, and the dyad of Sara and Andrea entered through its base. The low-lying mist of souls parted to grant them entry. Inside, the silver orbs of David, Prometheus, and Snake floated together at the center of the enclosed space created by the layers of fog and smog.

David greeted Thom and the others, and then called the meeting to order.

"As you all know by now," David said to the assembly, "we've succeeded in rescuing souls from the wells. We first freed their minds from their memory prisons, then we pulled their souls out of the monster, physically. This proves that Armageddon is not inevitable. We can defend ourselves."

"How do the soul wells fare now?" Buddha asked.

"We wounded them," David said. "But they've been harvesting in earnest. Alpha is now almost equal in size to Unum, and they are both bigger than ever before."

"How much bigger?" Thom asked. Distracted by his own issues, he'd left everything to David, including scouting the soul wells. David had stepped into the role like he was General Bradley. But it left Thom in the dark, a situation of Thom's own making. Now, he braced himself for the news of what the soul wells had become while he was wallowing in his own problems.

David reported, "When I first got here, you said the big one was five New York skyscrapers tall. Well, add another Empire State Building to that."

Thom felt his gut sink, even though he didn't have one. Around him, some of the souls and choirs shrank, their colors darkening.

"How did they grow so quickly?" asked the choir of Socrates.

"They've been staying in separate hemispheres," David explained, "gathering souls and keeping away from each other."

"And there are more people on Earth," Sara chimed in from her half of the dyad, "more souls available for them to feed on."

"That would explain why Alpha has been able to catch up," David said.

"Why haven't they been fighting?" asked a choir of World War I veterans. "They've always fought."

Confucius said, "Every time there was a disaster or a war. They'd gather and squabble like adolescent hyenas. This change is troubling."

Thom's imaginary gut sank further. He barely got his dad out. Corbin didn't make it out at all. And Lida was an exception of biblical proportions. Now the wells were bigger? Both of them!

"Here's the good news," David said, unfazed by the doubt radiating from everyone else, including Thom, "while they've been collecting more souls than they used to, more souls are escaping than ever before. Something must've changed on Earth, because more and more of us are reaching the surface and not fading."

Andrea dragged Sara to the center of the meeting and said, "We just came from down there and I can tell you atheism is on the rise. People aren't going to church like they used to."

"A lot of people say they believe," Sara added, "but they don't go to church or pray or even think about it much."

Andrea grumbled, "Except when they choose who to vote for...pretending the book they never actually read told them to hate the gays and love the billionaires."

Snake said, "That's remarkable news."

Prometheus added, "I've never seen a planet reject the propaganda of the soul wells. How could this have happened?"

"I told you this was the planet to end the endings," Snake said. "I told both of you. I wish Thor had stuck around to see this and to hear me say *I told you so*."

Ignoring Snake, Prometheus said to the assembly, "You have an opportunity to save your planet from the fate of all others. Thom and David have shown me what your species is capable of. For your sakes, for the sakes of all human souls, perhaps even for the sake of the universe, you must fight the soul wells."

Inching closer, Snake whispered to him, "You got your optimism back. I'm so happy for you."

Prometheus whispered back, "Don't hug me."

"What?"

"You heard me."

The billowing blue choir of Socrates said, "But even the totality of us can not measure up to the two monsters. As we speak, they acquire new souls."

"We're acquiring new souls too," Thom said. "Look around you. Look down. They rise through the ocean right now. And Andrea and Sara, they stand with us...I think, you do, right?"

"Of course," Sara said. "Though I don't speak for Andrea."

"Well," Andrea said, "you kind of do, in case you hadn't noticed the joined at the hip thing."

"I was being polite."

"Well," Andrea said, her half of their orb now a brilliant red, "stop being polite because I'm going back to war."

"You've been in a war," Lida gasped from above. "I hope the soldiers got you out of harm's way."

"No one got me *out*," Andrea said. "I was going *in*."

"Oh," Lida said, "were you a nurse?"

"I was a forward observer for artillery," Andrea said. "I got a Bronze Star and a Purple Heart...and two combat stripes."

"I wasn't in the service," Sara said. "We met after."

"This is a Council of War," David said, "not a luncheon. Sorry, Mom, I don't mean to be mean, but we need to discuss how to approach this. We need a plan."

"Yes, a plan," said a choir of World War II veterans. "We need a D-Day plan, not an Operation Torch disaster."

"But how can we stand against gods?" asked the red pinwheel choir of Confucius.

"We've stood against them twice now," David said. "And we won both times."

Socrates said, "The soul of the one called Corbin did not 'win' as you say."

"If you gaze long enough into the abyss," Nietzsche said, "the abyss also gazes into you."

"This abyss does not gaze," Socrates said, "it devours, and there's two of them, two ravenous gods."

"But they're not gods," Prometheus said. "And you must stop thinking of them as such. They are souls, greedy human souls."

"Yup," Snake said, "at the middle of those two big ugly things are a couple of souls just like each of you. Only they duped a bunch of other souls into surrendering their willpower, their living energy, to them. But at the middle of all that are two simple souls, and they're both real jerks."

"Even so," Confucius said, "would it not be wise for us to leave this planet the way Snake and Prometheus left their planets?"

"You would run?" Prometheus bellowed.

"We would save those who can be saved," Confucius said.

"How would this differ from yourselves?" Socrates asked. "You left your planet when it neared its end, did you not?"

"No," Snake said, his sphere swelling and growing a dark red, "I didn't leave by choice. I was thrown off by…by…"

"By the one he loved," Prometheus finished for his friend. "The one he loved exploded like the soul of Corbin." While Snake shrank into a ball of dark blue, Prometheus glowed red, his outer shell popping with sparks. He told them, "Snake's spouse went down to their living world, he went down during their Armageddon, and what he saw filled him with an anguish that swelled until he exploded. His name was Hasseree and Snake loved him. When he exploded, he threw Snake's soul into space."

Prometheus rose several yards into the air, his bright red light reflecting off the walls of fog around him. Even Buddha had been cast in tones of fury emanating from Prometheus.

"And me," Prometheus said, "I tried to save my spouse from our Armageddon. You have not yet seen such a thing. When those two monsters merge into one giant, the thing they become will be your Armageddon. And it will consume all of you, every single one, all of the souls across your afterlife, every choir, even the mighty Buddha. Then it will descend into the world of the living and suck the souls right out of their bodies until none remain. No more humans. No animals. No new souls of any kind."

"And you," Prometheus roared at Socrates and Confucius, "you would run? You would leave your world to that fate? When I faced the Armageddon of my world, I flew right toward it. I was one soul alone and I intended to attack the beast. I intended to save the one I loved, the only one…but he saved me instead. I tried and I failed. *But I tried.* Will you surrender your world without a fight?"

Silence wrapped the colorful gathering as Prometheus slowly lowered to the ocean's surface. He hovered beside Snake who, by some miracle, said nothing.

Then a great silver arm reached down and touched Prometheus. It was the choir majestic of Lida. "We are all so sorry for your loss," Lida said in concert with her many moms. "And for you too Snake. It is so kind of you to use your loss to help others."

"Thank you, ma'am," Snake said. "And Prometheus thanks you too."

"Yes," Prometheus said, slowly shrinking back into his normal silver self. "Thank you. You are very kind."

"That's what we're up against," David bellowed to the gathering. "That's what we have to save the world from. If we just lie down or walk away, then we doom the soul of every person who has ever lived. This is our time, our chance. It will be hell. Many will die. But this must be done, and we are the ones who must do it. Who is with us?"

The walls of the tower churned as the choirs and souls contemplated. While some, like Socrates, Confucius, and Nietzsche, slunk off toward the horizon, many others gathered closer to Thom and David. Only half of the gathering remained.

"It seems we have our answer," said the choir majestic of Buddha. "This is our army. What is our plan?"

The choir of World War I veterans asked, "Do we have a plan?"

"Thom has fought them and won," said Thom's detached choir. "He knows how to defeat the gods."

"I do have a plan," Thom said. "We'll do what David and I have already done, free souls from the wells. Each time we've freed a soul, it wounded the well and set others free. But this time I want us to pull out multiple souls at once."

"That sounds dangerous," Snake said. "What if multiple souls explode? It could be a different kind of end for all souls on Earth."

"It'll be dangerous for a lot of reasons," Thom said. "I'll stay back and direct the battle. If necessary, I'll call a retreat. Unlike before, there'll be no individuals, only choirs trying to save souls. I want a few choirs to volunteer to form connections with souls in Unum and only Unum. Then, we will wait for Unum to be at its weakest and attack."

"When is that?" Andrea asked.

Thom said, "When the soul well swims deeper or higher in the animalsphere. Also, when they open their mouth to feed. If we wait for Unum to be alone, low, and feeding, we'll have our best chance. This will be a probing attack. We're not out to kill Unum, not this time. This is simply a test of our tactics."

The choir of Druids asked, "What if Alpha attacks it?"

"That will only help us," Thom said.

"What if Alpha helps it and attacks us?" asked the choir of World War I veterans.

"Then I shall be our shield," Buddha said. "I will protect the choirs that attach to Unum. I'll block any attacks and give you shelter under my arms."

"Are you sure?" David asked. "When they hit each other, souls die. Every time it hits you, some of you will die."

"We know," said the collective voice of Buddha, "but it must be done."

"Time is not our friend," Thom said. "Any choir willing to be on the front lines, David and I will help you form a connection with a soul inside Unum. As for the rest of you, I could use all the reserves I can get."

The tower of souls and choirs dissolved and spread out. A handful of choirs gathered closer to volunteer to form connections. Seeing the dyad approach, Thom said, "Sorry, but two isn't really a choir."

"I understand," Sara said.

"But we'll stay close to you," Andrea said, "standing by as reinforcements."

Thom said, "Thanks, I'll probably need you when everything goes wrong."

Sara gasped, "When everything goes wrong?"

Thom explained, "In war, everything always goes wrong. Best to plan for it."

Seeing the choir majestic of Lida starting to depart, Andrea called out, "Where are you going? Aren't you joining the battle?"

"Oh, dear," Lida said, "war is a man's thing. Women don't play with guns and swords."

"Look at you," Andrea said, "you are a gun...a big fucking gun!"

"Language!" Lida exclaimed. "That is no way for a young lady to talk."

"I'm not a young lady," Andrea said. "I'm a warrior and a woman. And in that order."

"That's true," Sara mumbled. "Too true, especially in traffic."

Ignoring her, Andrea said to Lida, "Are you seriously going to stand back and watch while others who are weaker than you do battle—and just because you're a woman and they're men? Does that make sense to you?"

"Oh, I'd just be in the way, dear," Lida said, while David and the others stared on. "The men will do just fine without us. I believe in my David, and that Thom is a nice boy too. They know what to do."

Sara told Andrea, "She's from another time. I think you gotta let this go."

Andrea pulsed red. "If you won't join the battle, at least be close by. Stand with me and Sara. We're going to be with Thom, away from the fighting, just watching him direct things. Can you do that?"

"Of course, dear," Lida said. "I have to be there for my David."

"Yes," Andrea said, "you certainly do."

David said, "I don't need my mom chaperoning my battle."

Thom shushed him and changed the subject, moving on to who would be the attacking choirs. He didn't want to say it to David and spark more arguing, but they did need Lida chaperoning David's battle. A lot could go wrong. And like Andrea said, Lida was a gun, a big fucking gun. One Thom hoped he wouldn't have to deploy.

Chapter 16
A World Without a Dawn

Thom and David drifted together following Unum at a good distance but keeping it within sight through the murky gold fog. Far behind them, their army of choirs and free souls hovered on the horizon, waiting for the signal to advance. Four choirs, including Buddha, had connected to different individual souls within Unum. Now all they needed was a disaster or a war to entice Unum to gorge. Fortunately, and unfortunately, it was never long before the living had to face one or the other.

As Thom and David followed the gas giant cutting a vast wake through the gold deep below them, David said, "You know, this is the second time you and I stood together on the eve before a major battle. Not that we have 'eves' here; it's just one endless day."

"One endless night," Thom said, glancing up at the multi-colored specks that peppered the sky, each a life-bearing world, each facing the same possible end as Earth.

"Yeah, night," David said. "I think if I weren't dead, I'd go nuts. But that other 'eve' I was talking about, it was D-Day, on the docks. I was standing right next to you when we lined up for the transport."

"Sorry," Thom said. "I don't remember you there. I mean, I knew you were there, and every member of my team, but I don't remember you standing with me. I was…thinking."

"I know," David chuckled, his solid silver sphere shimmering as he did. "You were already climbing the cliffs in your head. I could see it in your eyes."

"I was a Staff Sergeant. It was my job to lead you guys through the mission. I had to be ready."

"And you were ready," David said, "just like you're ready for this."

But D-Day wasn't anything like this, thought Thom. He hadn't been in charge. He'd been under Sergeant First Class Williamson, as well as a Lieutenant, and there would have been a Major and a Lieutenant Colonel on the beach…if they lived. At Pointe du Hoc, Thom followed orders like David. But this battle rested entirely on Thom. And he had no choice; there was no one else who had succeeded in rescuing anyone, not even David. Lida rescued herself. Only Thom had ripped someone free by force.

Who knows how many other Stoneshields still suffered inside those wells? He couldn't walk away from that and the rest of the choirs and free souls that had asked him for leadership. They said they needed him, and Thom's dad agreed. And Thom agreed.

Feeling the totality of it, Thom wished he had a stomach so he could throw up. He reminded himself that this would only be a first battle, something to probe the limits of the soul wells and see what the choirs could do. There'd be other battles, other chances, at least Thom hoped so.

"You were a good leader because you were ready," David said. "You got killed real quick, but you were ready. Dying like that...it was just 'cause some Kraut got lucky."

"German."

"What?"

"Kraut is offensive," Thom said, remembering his conversation with Snake.

"So?"

"So, the war is over," Thom said. "It's been over. Stop calling them Krauts."

"You know what the fucking Nazis did right? What they did to me? To my dad? To my mom? You fucking know, right?"

"Yeah, I *fucking* know," Thom said. "But not every German who ever lived was a Nazi. So, if you wanna talk about Nazis, call them Nazis, not Krauts. And your mom wouldn't appreciate all the f-words either."

"Okay, fine," David said. "Some *Nazi* got lucky and killed you. It doesn't take away the fact that you're a good leader, Thom. That's what I'm trying to say. I'm just saying, I'm glad we have you leading the rest of us through this."

Thom hoped he was as ready as David thought he was. So many things could go wrong, things Thom could never imagine. He had to be ready for anything.

"Hey," David said, "Unum stopped."

"This might be it," Thom said.

As they watched, the oily black head of Unum rippled, pushing itself deeper into the golden haze, vanishing from sight.

"Now what?" David asked. "Go down for a look?"

"No," Thom said. "No need. We'll find out what this is in a moment."

As Thom expected, they didn't wait long before red, green, and blue souls surged to the surface. Some thick and already becoming clouds. Others thin and barely becoming puddles upon the ocean.

"A lot of people just died down there," Thom said. "This is our chance."

David grew a tentacle of fog and raised it in the air, signaling for the choirs to approach. A multi-colored stormfront drifted toward them.

"That thing you were saying before," Thom said, "about me being a good leader...thank you."

David glimmered. "I said it because it's true. Now, let's go give that false god a knuckle sandwich. Let's do this for Corbin."

"Yeah," Thom said, looking over the field of newly arriving souls, with more bubbling up each second, "but first let's see about evacuating these civilians."

***

The new souls told them there was a hurricane tearing up the coast of Mexico. Thom expected there to be many faithful for Unum to harvest. With Unum weakened by the effort of feeding and keeping itself submerged, this was the moment to attack. But first, Thom wanted as many non-combatants out of the area as possible.

Thom's dad and his ambulance corps quickly cleared the first wave of new arrivals. They gathered the weakest into halos before moving them to a safe distance. Those who could move on their own were guided away. As more surfaced, the corps of free souls and small choirs hurried them away as well. They gradually got ahead of the influx of refugees. It was almost safe to launch the attack.

David, Prometheus, and Snake stood with Thom as he watched the evacuation. Above him, four choirs waited for the order to attack—Buddha, the druids, a choir of World War I veterans, and another of World War II veterans. The WWII choir absorbed Thom's detached and much smaller choir of veterans dating back to the Battle of Dunbar. Together they had gathered around the silver sphere of David, becoming David's detached choir for this operation. Thom would remain a free soul with no choir, directing the fight.

As Thom waited for the ambulance corps to clear most of the new souls, Snake said, "Didn't you send a bunch of free souls off with Andrea and Sara?"

"Yeah, they're scouting for Alpha."

Prometheus said, "Then why does Andrea and Sara return with no free souls, only Lida?"

Thom turned to find the dyad approaching with the Choir of Lida hovering above them.

Drifting out to meet them, Thom asked, "What happened to your unit?"

"We followed your instructions," Andrea reported, "but there's no sign of Alpha. It must be on the other side of the planet."

"Andrea has you surrounded by a big ring of scouts or lookouts or whatever," Sara said.

"They're out as far as the horizon," Andrea said. "Everything is weird here—distance and time. So, I went out until I could barely see the big guy."

"Buddha," Sara interjected.

"Then I circled around, leaving a ring of lookouts behind," Andrea finished.

"You'll have plenty of warning if Alpha comes," Sara said. "But she wants to be here in case you need her."

"Okay," Thom said. "I might need you if we have trouble pulling free."

"A little extra muscle is always good," Andrea agreed.

"And we're here for moral support," the choir majestic of Lida collectively called down from above.

Then Lida called out alone, "Hi, David. It's your mom. Hi!"

"I know, Mom. Please, we need to start."

"Of course, David. You go ahead. I know you'll make me proud."

"And, Mom," David said, his silver sphere contracting, "I love you, Mom."

"I love you too, my big brave boy," Lida said, then drifted off toward a safe zone.

Andrea asked Thom, "Where do you want your extra muscle? What's the plan for us?"

Where would he need them and when? He wasn't sure. Mostly to himself, he mused, "This is only our first battle. It's something we'll learn from. It's just four choirs targeting four souls, and it's not like these souls are connected to the choirs the way I was connected to my dad, or like David was connected to his mom. I doubt we'll get them all out. And since Unum is much bigger than last time, and since Alpha hasn't been attacking Unum, I really don't know what'll happen. We're just going to have to be ready to learn and adapt and hope the next one goes better. So, I guess, be close and be ready for anything."

"Nice speech," Snake said, "way to rally the troops."

Andrea said, "So once again, I don't know what I'm getting myself into."

"What *we* are getting *us* into," Sara corrected her.

"Yeah…*us*," Andrea said, losing her bravado. "I think we'll go hang with Mrs. Lowenstein. If things go completely sideways, maybe I'll get her to step up. But don't count on it."

"Yeah, don't," Sara agreed.

As Andrea and Sara headed off, Thom called the choirs down to address his assault team.

"Remember," he told them, "stay together. The rally point is wherever Buddha is. Stay near Buddha. If I see any of you getting in trouble, I'll have Prometheus and Snake on hand to help. And Andrea and Sara are waiting in reserve. If we all get in trouble, I'll call a retreat. If I do, you'll have to let go of the souls you're trying to save, no hesitation. I promise, if this doesn't work, we will have other chances, but not if we all end up inside Unum, so obey the retreat order if it comes."

The Druids asked David, "Why doesn't the choir majestic of your mother join this battle?"

"It's not her way," Prometheus said before David could answer. "She sees war as a gender-specific ordeal."

"And it is," said the choir from World War I. "War is a man's responsibility."

"War is not for men or women," the Druids said. "All are affected."

"She's old-fashioned," David said. "She'll come around, maybe for the next attack. Just let her sit this one out."

Seeing the field of non-combatants mostly cleared, Thom said, "It's time to move out. David's choir will lead the way, followed by the World War I vets, then the Druids. Buddha will take up the rear and provide cover."

"And Thom, Snake, and I will be behind Buddha," Prometheus said.

"Let's show them what for," David said and dove into the golden ocean, his detached choir following close behind him.

The Druids and World War I choir followed David. Then the vast Buddha folded its arms behind itself and dove in next. Thom expected a splash and a wave, but Buddha made hardly a ripple.

Thom dove into the ocean next and was drawn down by the pull of Buddha's wake. Behind him, Prometheus and Snake stayed close. All around, the upward trickle of souls continued, the flow parting around Buddha. The black sky got farther away and harder to see, until it vanished behind the glittering veil of the ocean.

Thom soon heard the hymns, with their indistinct lyrics and melody. The sound mixed with the growing rumble of tentacles whipping through the gold to harvest the newly dead.

"Can you see Unum yet?" Thom called over the growing noise.

"Yes," Buddha said, "it's just coming into view. David is ordering us to stop here."

As they slowed, Buddha extended his arms out, restoring its broad pinwheel shape. Thom swam down and perched between Buddha's arms, riding their slow orbit around Buddha like a Ferris Wheel. Thom had expected to be met by David. Instead, he found David already extending a tentacle down to Unum. Though David's arm hadn't made physical contact yet, David's mind had receded from his soul, leaving his silver orb adrift. He was mentally gone, taking his detached choir with him.

"What the hell is he doing?" Thom demanded.

"He felt the connection," Buddha reported. "He said he had to go in now, while it was strong."

"That wasn't the plan," Thom yelled. "We're supposed to take this slow."

"The feast of souls won't last forever," said the veterans of World War I. "We should follow him, and quickly."

Unlike David, Thom took a second to review the situation. The swirling currents caused by Unum's swinging arm cleared the fog enough for Thom to see the monster. It now stood as tall as ten skyscrapers stacked one atop the other. Thom shuddered as he imagined that thing swallowing them all, even Buddha. He considered pulling everyone back to rethink this operation. But that would only give the soul wells more time to grow. And David's arm was almost about to touch Unum. Thom needed to decide.

"All of you," Thom said, "Let's do this. Let's save some souls!"

The Druids, the World War I veterans, and Buddha each extended an arm down to Unum. Before the others could catch up, David and his choir touched Unum. On contact, the soul well jerked, yanking David like a fishing bobber. The Druids made contact next, followed by the veterans. Buddha's arm made contact last. After David, Unum seemed to ignore the others, as if expecting them. Not a good sign, Thom thought.

"Can you hear me, Buddha?" Thom asked. "Are you still with me?"

"I am with you," Buddha said. "I am also with my choir who is with the young monk Seonji of Tibet. I am also with the Druids and the priestess Bangla-Shala, and with the choir of David and the hanging man Sergeant Rogers, and I'm with the veterans of the First Great War and the admirable Captain Bingham of the sky."

"How's it going?" Thom asked.

"It has only just begun," Buddha said.

Thom looked to Unum, expecting it to attack them with its tentacles. Instead, the monster ignored them and kept harvesting souls. Thom wondered what its plan was. Maybe it didn't want to fight them because defending itself did more harm than good? Maybe it was just hungry?

Over the rumbling air and endless hymns, Thom said, "Buddha, I want to go in through you, so I can see what's going on in there. If I go in and something happens out here, will you be able to pull me out?"

"I believe so," Buddha said. "As you said, this is new for all of us, so I cannot be certain."

"We'll take care of things while you're busy," Snake said, now hovering in the same space between the arms of Buddha, the two of them carried along on Buddha's Ferris Wheel. "If something happens out here, me and Prometheus will…I don't know…do something?"

"If something goes wrong," Prometheus said, joining them, "I will send Snake in after you while I supervise things out here. And if things go very wrong, I will order the retreat."

"And don't forget we have Andrea and Sara up there if we need them," Thom said. "And my dad; if you really need him, you can pull him off evacuation duty."

"If I'm in there getting you and he's out here running things," Snake asked, "then who goes to the surface to get reinforcements?"

"This is war," Thom said, "You'll have to improvise. Prometheus, I trust you to make the right decision."

"You trust Prometheus but not me?" Snake asked. "Good choice."

"Okay," Thom said, "I'm going in."

Thom touched Buddha's choir majestic and fell into the memories of the four choirs and their targeted souls.

***

Thom found himself in a plane, but it felt more like a kite. The thing was made of pipes and canvas. His head stuck out of the fuselage, with only a leather helmet and a pair of goggles to protect him. And he was flying. Fortunately, he knew how to fly, at least he did in this memory.

Hidden by canvas, his engine roared, sputtered, and smoked. But it seemed normal for a biplane. Thom realized he was inside the memory of Captain Bingham, the target of the World War I veterans. But Thom didn't sense them here, not yet. He felt only Bingham's adrenaline as he pushed his primitive aircraft through a hard turn.

There was a German ace out there. Bingham had chased him off the tail of a fellow Brit. Now the ace was trying get away from him, but Bingham's plane had a tighter turn radius. Engulfed by plumes of smoke rising from the frontline trenches, the captain could no longer see the German. But he could hear the German's engine. Every time his own sputtered, he'd hear it out ahead, winding to the left and climbing. Bingham knew that if he kept turning, as soon as they escaped the smoke, the ace would be in his gun sights.

The smoke thinned. But the German ace didn't appear. Someone else did, a fellow Brit, a new pilot, Lieutenant Felts. This was his second dogfight. The broad side of Felts' plane hung right in front of Bingham. He jammed the stick forward and to the right, but too late.

Bingham's right upper wing ploughed through the struts connecting the upper and lower wings of Felt's biplane. Then Bingham's nose slammed into the side of Felts' nose, knocking the engine block out the far side. The two planes merged into a single mass of twisted metal and flapping canvas.

As they spun toward the ground, the pilots stared into each other's eyes. In a matter of seconds, they'd both die on impact. Bingham had been too focused on getting the German, and now he'd killed himself. And worse, he'd killed this kid, barely eighteen.

"But you didn't kill me," said the kid as their planes continued to fall through the billowing smoke, far longer than it should've taken to reach the ground.

"It was my ego," said the soul of Bingham. "I wanted to shoot down that ace. I wasn't looking and I killed us both."

"It was low visibility," the kid said, but he wasn't the kid anymore. He was Lieutenant Hammond, a nineteen-year-old veteran, a man who'd served with Bingham, and a part of the choir of veterans. "You couldn't have seen Felts coming," Hammond said.

"You didn't kill him," the kid said, who was now another man who'd served with Bingham, twenty-year-old Captain March. "But you saved my life once. I got myself killed later, but you saved me."

Becoming Hammond again, the kid said, "And you saved my life twice."

"And mine," said a new face, a twenty-one-year-old Captain Tilden. "I lost count of how many times you chased a Gerry off my tail. I lived to see the Armistice because of you."

"Felts wasn't ready for a dogfight," Bingham lamented. "I was the commander. I should've been looking out for him, specifically him. I failed in my duty as his commanding officer."

While the tangled planes fell without end, Hammond, March, and Tilden took turns telling Bingham of the many times he'd saved them, or that they'd watched him save someone else. While a pilot's life expectancy was eleven days, Bingham's Little Circus had become top-heavy with veterans thanks to him. Now those veterans gathered to save Bingham's soul from Unum. Thom saw that it would take a little time, which was expected.

***

Thom focused on finding another memory and suddenly felt weapons and gear pulling down as a silk canopy pulled up; the harness between them squeezed around Thom. Above his head, heavy engines roared louder than any biplane ever could. Below, there was silence.

Thom had fallen into the memory of Staff Sergeant Rogers of the 101st Airborne Division. Below him was nothing but darkness. It was D-Day but not the way Thom had experienced it. While Rogers drifted toward the ground, Thom would've been somewhere out in the Channel, not yet in the landing craft.

Thom, as Rogers, slowly descended into the unknown. When the ground got close enough to see, it didn't look like the open fields they were supposed to land in. Instead, it was a small village in northern France. Thankfully, there was an open town square framed by a church, storefronts, a row of homes, and a low-walled graveyard. It spread before him, inviting him to land safely.

He descended in from the church side of the square, his chute guided by the fickle wind, with no say from Thom or Rogers. As he neared the square, he expected his momentum to carry him into the yards behind the row of homes across from the church, but his harness suddenly yanked him to a halt. He swung backwards and slapped against a brick wall with a grunt.

Once he had his wind back, Thom who was Rogers found himself hanging five stories above a tiled roof. His chute had caught on the steeple's cross, leaving him dangling below the steeple's bell. Around him were no windows, no decorations, nothing to get a hand on. Even the mortar between the bricks gave no purchase. He wouldn't be getting down without help.

As Rogers, Thom watched other soldiers descend over the square. One landed in the graveyard to his left while another came down hard in the square's center. Across the courtyard, three of his men landed on the roofs before their chutes dragged them into the backyards beyond. Others landed further on, but no more came down anywhere near the church. Rogers had a feeling he was going to be up there for a while. Even if someone spotted him, they wouldn't be able to get him down before securing the square.

After a few minutes, it was clear that none of the paratroopers who landed beyond the houses were coming back his way. And the one who landed hard wasn't moving. His chute fluttered across the square, bunching against the houses on the far side. It covered the doors and windows, flapping over the building's face.

The door behind the chute opened. Someone wrestled through the billowing cloth and tangled line. When they emerged, Thom saw two of them, both in Nazi uniforms, mostly. Their jackets weren't buttoned, and they didn't have their hats, but they did have their pistols.

As soon as they got free of the chute, they found the soldier attached to it, the trooper who lay motionless in the square. They shouted at him in German. The trooper came to and climbed to his knees, hands up.

Rogers searched for his own gun and found it dangling at the end of its tether, down below his feet, swinging near the wall of the steeple. Very carefully and quietly, he started pulling it up. It swung in and out, threatening to clap off the wall, bringing the attention of the Germans. But he kept pulling.

Down below, the American trooper remained kneeling with his hands up. The Germans kept barking at him, both at the same time. They disarmed him and knocked his helmet off. Then the Germans started arguing with each other and waving their guns at the sky and at the trooper.

As Rogers finally reeled in his gun, one of the Nazis pulled the paratrooper to his feet. Holding a wad of his coat, the German shoved his gun under the guy's chin, demanding answers.

Rogers lined his rifle up on the Nazi. At this range, even hanging like this, he could make the shot, he was pretty sure. His finger looped the trigger and held there, pressed against it but not pulling. If Rogers fired, he'd probably be dead before he could chamber and fire a second round. And the Nazis were yelling at the trooper, trying to get information, not looking like they were going to do anything else.

Then the trooper said, "Sorry, I don't speak no Kraut."

The Nazi fired. The trooper fell limp and the Nazi released him to the ground. Across the cobblestone spread a pool of dark red. Roger's eyes bulged. His heart thundered. He should've pulled the trigger. He could've saved that guy.

The other Nazi yelled at the shooter. But he stopped when a slight breeze wafted through the graveyard, lifting the chute that had come to rest there. The two Germans stopped barking at each other and hurried to the cemetery wall.

From his position, Sergeant Rogers could see the trooper hiding in the garden of headstones, and so could the Germans. He crouched behind the only monument big enough to give cover, a three-foot-tall block. The other markers were small and thin, worn by centuries of erosion. A bullet would probably shatter them.

Hunkered behind the wall, the Germans buttoned their jackets and whispered about how to flank the American. The trooper didn't seem to have his gun, and he definitely didn't have a way out.

Rogers, and Thom who was Rogers, raised his gun and fired.

The shot missed. The Nazis turned their guns on him, their pistol shots pinging off the bricks. Rogers chambered another round and fired, missing again. A bullet grazed his leg. Another hit him in the hip. Ignoring the pain, Rogers got off three more shots before he took a bullet in the neck.

The gun fell from his hands. He gripped the wound, but it did no good. Blood gushed down his throat and into his lungs. As he drowned in his own blood, he watched the Nazis jump the wall and run at the trooper, coming at him from both sides. The Nazis emptied their pistols into him before he could even flinch.

Then the square, the Nazis, and the dead paratroopers all faded behind blackness. Kneeling in a silent nowhere, Rogers wept.

Out of the nothing emerged two American paratroopers, each with a Screaming Eagle on his shoulder. Though he couldn't see their faces while he'd been hanging from the steeple, Rogers recognized them both—Sergeant Brooks who'd been pinned down in the graveyard and Corporal Lewis who'd been killed in the town square, both members of the choir of David.

"I'm so sorry," Rogers said.

"For what?" Lewis asked.

"I let you die," Rogers sobbed. "I should've shot them."

"You tried," Brooks said. "You were swinging up there. Did you even notice that the breeze had you moving a little? That shot was impossible…but you tried anyway. You tried knowing it'd get you killed. Not saving us doesn't make you any less a hero."

Lewis said, "You did what you could. That makes you a hero."

"I hesitated," Rogers said. "I should've fired sooner. I shouldn't've missed."

From behind Rogers, someone new grabbed Thom by the shoulder, and only Thom. The someone pulled Thom to his feet, leaving Rogers kneeling and weeping where he was. Thom turned to find that the someone was David.

Thom asked, "Where are we?"

"It's where Rogers is now," David said. "This is his own little hell. He just sits here crying about not pulling that trigger sooner."

Thom looked back to Rogers, his shoulders rolling, Brooks and Lewis standing over him in the darkness. "He couldn't have known they'd execute Lewis like that."

"I know," David said. "He knows it too. But he's been in here a long time, thinking about nothing else. Getting him out is going to take a little effort."

"You sure you can help this guy? This seems like a tough one and you only have Brooks and Lewis in here."

David said, "Don't worry about this. We got it. You go check on the Druids or Buddha."

"You sure?" Thom asked, gazing around the nothing. "This place...it's pure hopelessness."

David took Thom by both shoulders and turned him away from Rogers. "I have this, Thom. And I can keep an eye on the other veterans' choir, too. You go check the others."

David shoved Thom forward a step, out of Rogers' personal hell, and into sunlight.

Chapter 17
Crossing Lines

As dawn crept over the horizon, Thom stood on a hill overlooking a village of grass huts. A complex and ill-planned collection of furs draped his body. Dried, grey-blue mud covered his feet and legs up to the knee, as well as his face and neck. Feathers protruded in all directions from his tangled nest of hair. Then Thom realized that he was a woman, which was new and weird. But it was also unimportant to why he was here. In the village below him, every hut quietly slept, except one. Smoke curled from the roof hole as a young mother wailed within, a dirge for the child that had not lived through the night.

But the woman on the hill, the woman who was Thom, did not cry. She stared down in silence. She was the village healer, but nothing she'd done had saved the child. None of her herbs, none of her chants or prayers did anything for the infant. She started to wonder whether anything she'd ever done had helped anyone.

Before Thom could learn more about this lost child, another hand pulled him out of the woman's body and back into his own, wearing his D-Day uniform once again but still in the memory. The woman stood close in front of him but didn't seem to know he was there. Thom turned to see who had pulled him out. He expected to see David, or perhaps Snake, but instead it was someone he didn't recognize, a man with full cheeks, long ears, and dark hair tied up in a bun. He wore an orange robe over one shoulder. The other shoulder remained bare and bulging with muscle, just like his arms, neck, and every other part of the man.

Thom asked, "Who are you?"

The muscular man in the orange robes chuckled. "I guess you don't recognize me without the choir."

"Buddha? But those statues…"

"Yes, I know." Rubbing his belly, Buddha said, "Those statues actually confuse me with another fellow; I don't mind them. But it would've been rather difficult to become so rotund when I had to carry my water so high up a mountainside every day."

"Why didn't you move closer to the water?"

Buddha chuckled again. "Then I wouldn't have had to carry water so far, and I would not have obtained a balance within myself."

"Balance?" Thom said. "Like balancing two buckets on a pole, not spilling them, or something?"

"Or something," Buddha said. "That is not the balance I speak of, though one kind of balance can bring the other. Perhaps when this is over, I will teach you. But this is not why I am here now."

"Yeah, why are you here? That's Bangla-Shala, the priestess. This is supposed to be the Druids helping her. Why are you here?"

"I came for you."

The scene around them changed from a hilltop into a mountainside. Thom realized they were both hanging in midair, yet he felt solid ground under his feet. A young man in orange robes sat on a mat spread on a small outcrop of rock. Below, a different village quietly slept as the sun rose behind mountains on the far side of the arid valley. The huts of this village were made of ornately carved wood, painted crimson and detailed in blue. Exactly how it was detailed was impossible to see from this far up. The outcrop had to be at least twenty stories up the face, and the mountainside was almost a vertical wall. It had features that maybe a mountain goat could climb, but not a man. Thom couldn't imagine how the young monk had reached this spot.

"This is where I am with my choir," Buddha said. "This young man is Seonji. He is sacrificing himself to the universe to end a long drought that has claimed the lives of many villagers. He will meditate here until he dies of exposure."

"Will that work? Does sacrificing himself end the drought somehow?"

"Of course not. Our spirits cannot control the weather. But our spirits do heal each other." Buddha sat down in midair, facing the young monk, mirroring his position. "He is sad because he failed to end the drought through meditation. Focusing on outcomes is not the way to nirvana. This misunderstanding led to the sadness that Unum uses to trap him here. But we will show him the value of his sacrifice, as well as the error in his understanding."

"But his death didn't end the drought," Thom said.

"No, it did not," Buddha said. "However, it did have value. After he dies here, his body will go undiscovered on this mountainside for decades. It will remain sitting as he does now, slowly drying into a natural mummy. When the descendants of those villagers find him, they place him in a shrine where he is worshiped for his sacrifice. He becomes a symbol that brings the community together in times of need. His sacrifice did not end the drought, but it did bring together the descendants of his village." Buddha turned his smile to Thom. "It will not be hard to show him the good he did."

"So, you brought me here to tell me you can rescue him?"

"He can rescue himself," Buddha said, "but I did not bring you here for that. I brought you here so you could know each of our four memories before I send you back. The battle against the dark one has had an unexpected turn. Prometheus has asked for your presence."

"But—"

With a bow of his head, Buddha threw Thom out of the memory.

Thom emerged into his soul, a bright red, spherical cloud hovering below Buddha's choir majestic. The silver sphere of Prometheus hovered beside Thom. Below them, David and the other three choirs had gathered close to Buddha for cover.

Though most of Unum's focus remained on gathering the diminishing trickle of souls, it dedicated one arm to whipping the choirs. Thom watched as the black tentacle swung across the golden expanse, on course to strike the choir of veterans. But one of Buddha's arms curled in, taking the hit. Lightning fired from the impact. Unum's arm lurched back while Buddha shuddered. Then Unum drew back to strike again.

Prometheus bellowed over the thunder and hymns, "With each impact, a soul in Buddha's choir dies, but several souls would perish if the smaller choirs were stuck."

Now was not the time to mourn the lost, Thom thought. "Where's Snake?" he yelled over the sound of another impact hitting Buddha.

"He's bringing Andrea and Sara and anyone else who can help."

"Why? What's the problem?"

"Look." Prometheus pointed a tentacle down toward the maelstrom.

Deep below, Unum frantically undulated to keep itself submerged. The crown of its giant round head bulged under the pull of the four choirs, each grasping a different soul. Everything appeared to be going according to plan. Then Thom looked again. David's choir was no longer David's. It left him to join the choir of World War I veterans. David fought to free Rogers alone.

Thom's soul swelled and flashed. "What the hell is this?"

Prometheus said, "The Great War veterans were having trouble with Bingham, so David sent his choir to help, saying he had Rogers, no problem."

Thom shrank and swelled. "Dammit, David. Why can't you—"

His words were cut short by a growing din from above. Thom turned to find the choir majestic of Lida cutting a broad wake through the gold. With her were Sara, Andrea, and Snake. They sped down and halted abruptly just above Buddha. The gushing wake of gold washed off Lida and swept over Thom and Prometheus.

"Where's David?" Lida begged. "Is he okay?"

Buddha told her, "Your son stands alone in a memory, but he is winning the soul of the one called Rogers."

Lida called to her son. "Are you okay? Why aren't you working with your friends? What happened?"

"I'm fine," David grunted.

"David?" Thom asked. "You're back?"

"Yeah," David said. His arm down to Unum was pulled tight. "I just got Rogers out of that memory. Now, I'm ready to pull him out of that monster. Why's my mom down here?"

"Why the hell are you alone?" Thom demanded. "Why isn't your choir helping you? Why are they with the other veterans?"

"They needed each other," David said, "but I didn't need nobody. I'm doing better alone."

"This was supposed to be a team working together," Thom barked at him, "not you going it alone."

David pulled and grunted, "What are you complaining about? We're winning."

Thom turned to Buddha. "Are we winning?"

"I have freed the young monk from his personal torment," Buddha said. "The Druids have saved Bangla-Shala. And the pilot, Bingham, is also escaping his memory. His mind will be free, but his soul and the other souls remain in Unum's grip."

Another whip struck Buddha, releasing more lightning. Over the thunder that followed, David yelled, "We can get these souls out, all of them. So, let's do it!"

Thom said, "Okay, but no more surprises, *David*."

"Be careful, David," Lida said as she tightened her choir's arms around herself. "Thom, is he being carful? Buddha, are you helping him? You should both be helping him."

"*You* should be in there helping him," Andrea said, her half of the orb glowing red.

"Yes," Sara agreed, her red catching up with Andrea's. "You're bigger than everyone, except Buddha. You need to join this fight."

Lida glowed back at them. "You two need to come away from there before someone has to rescue you."

Another tentacle struck Buddha, releasing more lightning and thunder. Before the rumble had dimmed, another swung in, forcing Buddha to use a second arm to block it. Then another and another. Lightning cracked and danced while one thunderclap rolled into the next. Under the relentless wave of whipping limbs, Buddha closed its arms around the smaller choirs, forming a protective cage.

"What the hell is happening?" Thom cried.

"The feast has ended," Buddha said. "The mouth of Unum has closed. We have its undivided attention."

"That's it," Snake said. "It's time to cut and run."

David snapped, "We can't leave these souls!"

"What about you?" Thom called to the smaller choirs. "Can you get them out fast?"

The Druids said, "We need more time, more strength."

"I almost have Rogers," David grunted as he pulled. "We can get them out, all four at once, if we merge into one arm pulling all four souls together."

"No," Prometheus roared. "You cannot combine the choirs. It would end your world."

"Not the choirs," David said, "just our arms. Combine all four tentacles and pull together. I mean, our arms are like smoke, right? We can merge the smoke, right?"

"I believe it would work as David describes," Buddha said.

"But that might pull the choirs together," Prometheus warned, over the roar of the continuous attacks. "You will all merge and become another soul well. Please, don't do this."

Thom contracted and expanded as he imagined a world with three soul wells, including one of his own making. Looking at those fighting beside him, he couldn't imagine any of them becoming such a monster. Then he looked to Prometheus and wondered if he had the same thought just before Alpha formed.

Thom said, "Okay, combine the limbs, *not* the choirs."

"Please, no," Prometheus begged, but it was already too late.

David swept his overstretched arm into that of the veterans, and then into that of the Druids. The three limbs fused into a single tentacle of thick red smoke, buzzing with sparks. David swung the combined limbs into Buddha's, creating one, bright red tentacle that glowed all the way down to where it vanished inside Unum.

"On my word," Thom yelled, "everyone pull together!"

Thom counted and they heaved. As the shared arm stretched, it glowed brighter and brighter. The light filled the animal souls around it. Miniature golden versions of their Earthly selves—deer, falcons, whales, and others—burst into existence and then ran, jumped, swam, and swooped around the line. Still, Unum held onto the four freed souls.

Thom ordered, "Again."

Before they could, one of Unum's tentacles dodged Buddha's defenses. It slipped inside the cage of arms and wrapped itself around David's silver orb. David went limp. His connection to the merged limb dissolved.

Before Thom realized what was happening, the invading tentacle dragged David down. Lida screamed. Thom quickly created an arm and grabbed him. With all his strength, Thom swam against Unum, but it was useless. The dark limb wrenched them downward. The gold gurgled around Thom. He and David plummeted, beyond the Buddha's protection.

"Help!" he cried.

Prometheus quickly wrapped a silver tentacle around Thom. Thom and David jolted to a stop. Unum continued to pull. Prometheus frantically swam up, wide ripples rolling down his silver orb body. Together, Thom and Prometheus swam upward through the golden haze, dragging David with them, lifting him back into the safe harbor of Buddha's arms.

"That's good, Prometheus. Keep going. I think Unum is weakening."

"I won't let the soul well take you," Prometheus declared. "But I believe Unum has trapped David's mind. He is in a memory of his own."

Lida called from behind Buddha, "Promise me you won't leave my boy in there."

"I'll get him out," Thom said. "I promise."

Andrea said to Lida, "Why aren't *you* getting your son out?"

Lida gasped. "I couldn't possibly."

"Seriously, you need to stop this bullshit," Sara said.

"Language, young lady."

"Are you fucking kidding me," Andrea said. "We're at war here. Stop worrying about bad words and do something!"

"That's enough," Thom barked at them. "I need all of you out of here. If you're not a part of this fight, I need you on the surface, helping my dad."

Snake paused, his shell becoming a deep, dark green. "I'm staying...to help. Oh my, I actually said that. Well, I guess I'm doing it. I'm staying to help, Thom."

"Not this time," Prometheus said.

Snake said, "But someone has to—"

"I almost lost you once already," Prometheus cut him off. "I cannot bear to go through that again."

Growing brighter, Snake said, "Since you put it that way, okay. But be careful, please."

"Yes, my friend, I will be careful...for you."

"You said *my friend*." Snake glowed pink. "And you were talking to me."

"Yes, Snake, you are my friend," Prometheus said. "Now, withdraw from this place while you can."

"I love you too, Prometheus."

Prometheus sighed.

"That's enough," Thom yelled. "Everyone out of here, now! Lida, get them out of here, please."

"Of course, dear," Lida said, her voice shaky. She scooped up Snake, Andrea, and Sara. "I know you won't let anything happen to my David, Thom," she said before she slowly drifted toward the surface.

"How shall we proceed?" Prometheus asked as he continued to inch them higher within the protection of Buddha's arms.

David's mind was still inside that monster. If they cut David's connection to it, Thom wasn't sure what would happen. And he knew this was unlike anything Prometheus had done, so he didn't know either. "I'm guessing we'll have to free his mind before we can get him out," Thom said.

"That's an appropriate assumption."

"Let me free the others first," Buddha said. "I believe I can help the other four free themselves the way Lida freed herself and the moms. Helping them should wound Unum, making it easier for you to rescue David."

"Okay," Thom said, not sure what Buddha meant to do. "I trust you. Let's free those souls!"

Thom still expected the choirs to pull the trapped souls out of Unum. Instead, they went silent, and their merged tentacle relaxed. Before Thom could question this, the hazy silver arms of Buddha's cage thickened from a fog into a glittering metallic fluid. This transformation to liquid silver spread down Buddha's tentacle to where it merged with the arms from the smaller choirs. The silver transformation flowed up their arms and into the choirs themselves. Almost instantly, they each became a silver sphere of liquid metal like Prometheus, but many times larger.

Prometheus said, "How is Buddha doing this?"

Thom said, "I was going to ask you."

The silver transformation continued down the shared limb of the choirs, spreading toward Unum. In the animalsphere that surrounded the glowing limb, more animal souls regained their Earthly forms. They became life-sized gold versions of themselves and raced off into the haze in a steady exodus of every kind of animal.

The slinking silver reached the crown of Unum's head and entered. The dark monster shuddered and contracted. Though it kept its grip on David, its other seven tentacles pulled in tight under its massive round head. The monster convulsed, yanking David down as it did. Thom and Prometheus swam against it, their bodies rippling in time with each other. Together, they barely held their ground.

Thom cried to Buddha and the others, "We're slipping! Pull now! Hurry!"

"There's no need," Buddha said. "We shall free the souls without physical force."

"How?" Prometheus asked but he received no answer, only a hum.

The calming, hypnotic hum emanated from every part of Buddha and then from the smaller choirs as well. The sound moved down the shared tentacle to the soul well. Unum's indistinct hymns became an agonized wail. The shared arm brightened until it glowed white. Herds and flocks of silver animals sprang into existence and scattered away. The arm grew even brighter and the hum ever louder.

The noise and light pressed in on Thom, assaulting his senses, rattling his mind. It felt as though it would burrow into his soul and change him like it changed the small choirs, a change toward that Nirvana thing. Though he still didn't understand what it was exactly, Thom knew it was good. But he also he wasn't ready for it. He needed to change somehow before it would "work" for him. Emotionally, he walled it out. Still, it pressed in. Thom felt his barricade ready to crumble under the hypnotic hum and uplifting light. He was about to break.

Then it all stopped.

Chapter 18
The Final Darkness

As the light receded, Thom found himself hovering in the golden haze, surrounded by the liquid silver arms of Buddha. Beside Thom, the two smaller choirs—the veterans and the druids—remained a pair of silver orbs, with no arms extending from them. Thom's arm still held onto David, and Prometheus still held onto Thom. Deep below, Unum offered only passive resistance to Thom and Prometheus as it hung adrift, its one tentacle wrapped around David, the other seven limp and lifeless.

"What happened?" Thom asked. "Where are the four souls we were rescuing?"

Buddha said, "We meditated together—the choirs, the trapped souls, and myself. The priestess and young monk helped greatly."

"And?"

"We succeeded. The four souls achieved self-realization. They became Unum's indigestion, much more so than Lida and the moms."

Thom didn't get it. Buddha was telling him that they'd won while it looked like they'd lost. He asked, "But where are they? And what about the soul well? Is it dead?"

Buddha said, "Watch and we will learn the answer together."

Thom kept watching, waiting, growing impatient, until a beam of light broke through the crown of Unum's giant bulbous head. The light was slender, silver, and bright. Unum shuddered as the beam moved, cutting a jagged line across it head. The wound widened and split. Unum's black shell peeled back like rose petals, revealing a luminous core. The monster melted into a nebulous cloud of silver and black. From the silver, souls of red, green, blue, and gold dripped upward like a gentle summer rain. Some hit the closed arms of Buddha, dripped around them, and continued falling up. From the black parts, eight thin tentacles reached out to regather the escaping souls. When they caught one, the drop would slip from its grasp and rise away.

Four of the ascending souls guided themselves into the cage of Buddha. They paused before Thom, each a silver ball about half the size of Prometheus. They stared at Thom while he stared back. The mercury arms of Buddha and the steady rise of rainbow rain were draped behind them. Though Thom saw no gesture and heard no words, he knew them to be the monk Seonji, the healer Bangla-Shala, the pilot Captain Bingham, and the paratrooper Sergeant Rogers. Thom felt them express gratitude before they rejoined the upward migration.

As more and more souls escaped, Unum's indistinct hymns grew thin and ghostly. Still, the arm holding David remained rooted as if anchored in cement.

"The soul well is undone," Buddha said, "broken into a cloud, but it still lives."

Prometheus said, "Unum could still reform, but it would be much weaker. This has been a victory. We need only free David and retreat."

They'd won the battle, but not the war, not yet. Prometheus was right, they only needed to get David's mind out of that thing and make a run for it. Thom said, "I'll get him out of that memory. Prometheus, I need you to keep us from being pulled down."

"Let me go in and save David," Buddha said. "My soul is in balance. I can bring his into balance, as well."

"No, the memory he's in, I've been there before. And I'm not sure he'd take to whatever you just did for those other guys. I have to go in this time."

Before Buddha could protest further, Thom focused his mind and fell into the memory holding David. Thom found himself exactly where he thought he would—back at that prison holding David's dad. But it was different this time. There was no train, no dirt path, no Rabbi Cohn. It was just the prison yard and a handful of guards scattered around its parameter. They watched over a cluster of whimpering children gathered around a single adult, David's father. Only this wasn't David's memory of him. It was Abraham's soul trapped inside Unum.

Abraham Lowenstein wore the same black suit, his long beard, and a yarmulke. He radiated blue—deep, dark, and cold. Around him, the children radiated nothing; they were but grey memories, a bleak manifestation of Abraham's thoughts. His hands reached out to the shadow children, as if it were possible to ease their fear, their sorrow, their anger. And just like when he was still alive,

Abraham's thoughts were trapped in the moment that started this nightmare.

When he'd first arrived, Abraham had been dragged over to a young officer, who'd said, "You are the mohel, yes? That means you are good with children, yes?"

And Abraham had nodded.

"Good, good," the officer said.

The words became locked in his brain. They could not be excised. They'd replayed over and over as Abraham had to lead the children from his own synagogue to the tiled room. The words kept playing when he slept, when he ate, when he led more and more children across the muddy yard.

After the allies had reached his camp, freeing them from the Nazis, they tried to take care of Abraham. He lay in a field hospital, the doctors doing all they could, but the words would not stop. They droned on and on until finally they droned the life out of him.

And the words continued, following him into the afterlife, following him to here, where they imprisoned him, and now they imprisoned his son. The horror of all those moments piled upon each other crushing down on Abraham, crushing down on David. Now that he was in the memory with them, they crushed down on Thom. He heard the words, repeating over and over, the two syllables that defined Abraham's personal hell.

"*Gut, gut.*"

All those moments poured through Abraham's mind, and thus through David's and Thom's, while they walked a group of children toward the heavy airtight door, a walk that never ended, or even got any closer. They just kept walking and walking, the children with them, the guards and the buildings around them, all out there in an unreachable wall of haze.

Thom gazed at the children. He recognized them but not from his own memories; they were from Abraham's and David's. They were the children of their synagogue.

A transformation swept across the gathering like wind over wheat. As it passed, every face became the face of David Lowenstein. They were all different Davids at different ages, but they were all David. Then the wind shifted, and the children from their synagogue were back with their own faces. And back and forth they changed in slow sweeps, between the Davids and all the others, forever walking toward the tiled room behind the airtight door.

Thom shook it off. He needed to reach David. Taking control of the memory for as much as he could, Thom yelled, "David! David, can you hear me?"

The memory continued to play out around him, the changing faces, the never-ending march, that young officer's words.

Thom fought through it, refocused his will, and cried, "David! I need you!"

He could feel David inside the memory, his thoughts drowning in his father's dread. Around them, the children's faces became that of David, staring up at Thom with their long, grey eyes. Thom wanted to look away, but he forced himself to stare into the eyes of the Davids. He stared until the gloom lost its power over him.

"David," Thom called again, forcing calm into his mind. "I need you to focus and talk to me. Please, David."

Thom waited, hoping to sense that his friend had at least heard him. He did sense something but not David. From the haze of the surrounding prison yard, one of the guards walked toward Thom. Unlike the eternal march of condemned children, the guard closed the distance with each step.

"Yea, though I walk through the valley of the shadow of death," said the SS camp guard, "I will fear no evil."

Thom squinted at the hazy figure. "Peterson?"

A chill ripped through Thom as his gaze fixed upon Peterson in an SS uniform. Driven by fury, Thom stepped out of the memory of Abraham and through the mist of false children, the memories parting like fog round him.

Back in his D-Day uniform, he marched over to meet Peterson. Thom roared at him, "How could you wear that uniform?"

"Yea, though I walk through the valley of the shadow of death," Peterson repeated, "I will fear no evil."

Thom could feel his face boiling red as he growled, "You're wearing evil. This place is evil. You serve evil!"

"Treasure the Lord's gracious love. Walk humbly in the company of your God."

Peterson came into sharp focus while the memory of the concentration camp faded into grey mist. Thom felt himself drifting away from David and his father. They vanished behind the gathering fog, moving farther and farther away. He could feel something coming...or was Thom moving toward it? He couldn't be sure.

As the mist flowed around him, Thom demanded, "Where are you taking me?"

"The Lord is my shepherd," Peterson said with a broad smile.

"That doesn't answer my question."

Peterson's smile twitched. "God works for the good of those who love him, who have been called according to His purpose."

"Your lord is a lie, Peterson. There is no god, only propaganda."

"Trust in the Lord with all your heart and lean not on your own understanding; in all your ways submit to Him."

Thom grabbed Peterson by the lapel of his Nazi uniform. "I submit to nothing, and neither should you. You're being a chump. Don't let the soul well do this to you. I can get you out. Me, you, David, and Abraham, we can all get out together."

Peterson stared back at Thom, his smile steady and vacant, just like his wide eyes. Under Thom's grip, the stiff wool of Peterson's SS coat became black cotton robes. Thom released him and turned to find a room forming around him. The fog became polished wood benches arranged in rows. A stone wall rose behind them.

"What is this?"

"The Lord your God is with you, the Mighty Warrior who saves." Peterson now sat behind a tall wooden bench. He wore black robes and a powdered wig. Beside Peterson, in a lower seat, sat an elderly man, his face in shadow. Still wearing his D-Day uniform, Thom found himself fenced in by a waist-high wooden railing. He was centered before the bench and between the bench and the empty gallery.

"Is this a court?" Thom scoffed. "I'm the defendant, of course. And who's that with you up there?"

Peterson slammed a gavel. "A good man leaves an inheritance to his children's children, but the sinner's wealth is laid up for the righteous."

The elderly man leaned forward into a dusty beam of grey light. Thom instantly recognized the leathery visage of his war-worn grandfather.

"You killed our name," his grandfather declared. "You married no woman. You fathered no child. You desire to be of Sodom and Gamora, to commit sins of the flesh. You were a fruit, a nance, a *blue discharge.*"

Thom laughed at Peterson's failure to understand the scripture he was weaponizing. "What sins of the flesh? Sodom and Gamora was about kindness to strangers, your duty to guests in your home. And I wasn't discharged...and whose idea of a military court is this because it certainly ain't mine. What are you going for, drama?"

"Honor thy father and thy mother!" Peterson slammed the gavel again.

"Look, jackass, I don't think that's really my pops and I don't feel guilty about who I was, not anymore. But mostly, I don't have time for this crap. I have a friend who needs me."

Thom turned away from the bench and gazed hard at the empty gallery. Out there, beyond it, he could feel David's consciousness.

"You killed our family! You killed the name of Stoneshield!"

Thom shut out the angry shouts ringing from his grandfather and focused only on the connection he'd made with David, his friend, a soul that needed him. The floor beneath the empty seats shook and rolled. The walls cracked. The ceiling rained plaster.

"Honor your father and your mother, so that you may live long in the land the Lord your God is giving you!"

"Keep your lousy lord land," Thom growled.

The back wall of the gallery exploded into debris, revealing a spinning vortex of black and grey that sucked the wreckage away. Bolts of black lightning fired across the vortex and into the crumbling courtroom.

"Those who hope in the Lord will renew their strength," Peterson cried over the thunder and roaring wind. "They will soar on wings like eagles! They will run and not grow weary! They will walk and not be faint!"

Thom turned and stared Peterson in the eye. "Your lord is a selfish jerk. He doesn't give. He only takes."

What remained of the courtroom burst into burning splinters that swirled into the growing vortex. Only the judge's bench and witness stand remained, surrounded by dark fog, lightning, and thunder.

Thom kept his glower fixed on Peterson and his thoughts fixed on David. He focused, forcing the memory to go where he wanted to be. Slowly, the roar of wind and thunder faded. The fog thinned. The witness stand with Thom in it and the bench with his grandfather and Peterson, all floated down until they came to rest on solid ground. They were once again inside the concentration camp.

Behind Thom, surrounded by the vague forms of Nazi guards, the memory of Abraham walked the children toward the gas chamber, never reaching it. Before Thom, Peterson and Thom's grandfather sat together as judges, casting contempt upon him. Thom continued to stare at Peterson, ignoring the specter of Thom's grandfather, knowing it to be an illusion. He stared until the figment of his grandfather faded into fog and drifted into the air.

Thom sneered. "I knew that wasn't my pops. My pops wouldn't've sat there through all your crap. He was crabby, but he loved me, his only grandson. So, I think he'd've socked you right in the mouth."

Peterson started to respond but Thom had had enough of bible quotes. With a wave of his hand, Peterson's words no longer reached his ears. While Peterson's mouth flapped silently from high upon the bench, Thom vanished the witness stand from around himself. Then he walked over to the children. They were mere figments like his grandfather but, no matter how hard he focused, he couldn't vanish them or the guards or anything else in this memory. They were not his to vanish. Nor did they belong to David.

Thom stopped at the edge of spectral children. "David!" he screamed into the memory of Abraham. "David! Can you hear me!"

"I can hear you," a voice said from above.

In the murky sky above the camp appeared a head that didn't look human. It had a long face with tall, black eyes. In place of a nose, it had two long flap-covered slits. Its mouth seemed very human. And its skin was soft and human-like as well, though its color was a light beige unlike any skin tone Thom had ever seen. Topping the earless head was a crest of brown downy fur.

Thom had never seen such a thing, but he somehow recognized it. "Prometheus? Is that your face…I mean, your face from when you were alive?"

"Yes," boomed the head of Prometheus in the sky, "but that is unimportant now. I have come to warn you. There are dire conditions rapidly progressing toward cataclysm. You need to free David from this memory quickly."

"Why? What's happening out there?"

"Alpha is here," Prometheus reported, "and it has consumed Unum."

"Consumed?" Thom bellowed. "Are you saying Alpha ate Unum?"

"Drank would be more correct," Prometheus said. "Alpha opened its vortex of a mouth and drew in the nebulous remains of Unum. The Armageddon of Earth has formed. It now holds David's body and your mind."

"Who is with Buddha besides us?" Thom said.

"Lida has returned with the dyad, Andrea and Sara. Snake is there too. But even with Buddha's help, we cannot hold on for long. Your planet is lost. We must save those we can. You need to get David and yourself out quickly…if you can get David out at all. Look."

Prometheus gestured toward David still inside the memory of Abraham. While Thom had been dealing with Peterson and Prometheus, David had turned a dark and sparkling blue. Overloaded with emotion, David had become a bomb, like that German boy, and like Snake's spouse had been.

"No," Thom said, "this is not the end of Earth. It's the end of Alpha. Go back and tell the others that I'll be out soon, and I'm bringing David with me. There will be no Armageddon here."

Prometheus started to protest but stopped. Instead, he said, "I hope that your words prove true." He vanished from the sky.

Thom turned to the silently blustering Peterson. With a wave of his hand, Thom transformed him and his bench into smoke. It drifted away. Thom turned back to David and strode into the mist of children. He stood amongst them, disrupting three mournful Davids, reducing them to pillars of formless fog.

"It's not real David!" he called into the memory of Abraham. "Don't let it hold you!"

He received no answer.

David affected the memory of Abraham, turning him dark blue as well. From them, dark bolts fired in random arcs, burning away children only to have them reform a moment later.

Thom glowed red. He wanted to reach in and rip David from that nightmare. He wanted to do something physical, but it didn't work that way here. There was another way to reach David, the way that Buddha rescued the four souls without force. Thom wasn't clear on the details, but he had the general idea. He did what he thought would make it work.

Thom unclenched his fists, lowered his head, and closed his eyes. Breathing soft and steady, he focused on his friend and how his friend needed him, just like he'd done when David had arrived in the afterlife, when he was on the edge of fading away. The red light emanating from Thom dulled and a new gold light glowed through it.

"David?" Thom said softly, as he projected gold into his friend's consciousness. "Can you hear me, David?"

"Thom!" The word came smothered in rumbling winds. "It hurts!"

Thom shivered at the sound as if a chilled wind had carried it to him. Though David's soul was right there in front of Thom, David felt a million miles away. Thom stepped closer, his gold shining upon the memory and the soul of Abraham, feeding strength into him and David. Thom could only hope it would work in here like it worked out in the cloud world.

"Feel the light," Thom called. "Take strength from it. Use it to break free."

"It's too late!"

"No, it's not!" Again, his instincts told him to reach in and pull David out. But he knew it wouldn't work. He'd be more likely to be pulled into the nightmare with David. Thom had to stay calm and keep doing what Buddha had done. He tried to calm himself and focus.

"Listen to me," David cried. "My dad is in here and it's like we're fused. The blue lightning isn't me; it's him. And it's getting worse. My father is going to explode like Corbin."

Thom said, "Alpha ate the rest of Unum. It's the Armageddon. I need you, David. We all need you."

Still lost behind wild winds unfelt by Thom, David yelled, "Get out of here, Thom. Get out, let my soul fall into Alpha, and get everyone as far away as you can. If we explode in here, I'm sure we'll kill it. Tell my mom I love her."

Thom's gold faded into blue. David's plan would probably work, Thom expected. But he couldn't leave David to sacrifice himself. He wasn't going to leave a man under his command behind. "No. We can get you out. We can get you both out and kill Armageddon together."

"No," David said firmly. "My father and I will kill Armageddon. You have to help everyone else, Thom. Leave the memory, go back out there, and let go of me. Make everyone let go. Let me fall in so I can explode with my father. We'll destroy the Armageddon from the inside out. Leave, Thom. And tell my mom I love her. And goodbye."

"No, David! You don't have to do this!"

Without answering, the soul of David faded back into the memory of Abraham, beyond Thom's reach.

Thom darkened into blue. He couldn't let David die in here like this. He wouldn't.

"I'm leaving," Thom said, though he knew David couldn't hear him. "But I'm not abandoning you."

Thom needed to go out there and find a way to save David, save everyone. He closed his eyes and focused on himself and his own physical soul. When he opened his eyes again, he had escaped the memory. He was in his cloud body, strung between David's unconscious orb below and the orb of Prometheus above. With one arm, Buddha kept Prometheus, Thom, and David from being pulled in while its other arms sheltered them from the whipping tentacles of Alpha-turned-Armageddon.

Looking down into the swirling golden haze, Thom found no trace of Unum. There was only Alpha, now as tall as twenty New York City skyscrapers, one atop the other. A chill ripped through him. They could barely fight that thing now. If he rescued David and allowed it to live, to feed, to grow even larger, unchecked by Unum, there'd be no chance of stopping it. They would all die. And abandoning the Earth to run away? Thom couldn't. He had to do something here and now, but what? The only plan he could think of was the one David was already executing—suicide from within.

"Thom," Lida said from behind Buddha. "Where's David? Why aren't you helping him?"

Thom's spherical cloud turned a deep, dark blue. They had to kill Armageddon now or they never would. He had no choice. "I'm so sorry, Mrs. Lowenstein. I've done all I can."

Her entire choir darkened. "No…please, no…"

"I need you to do something for me," Thom said to Lida. "Tell my dad that I love him, and that he was a good father."

Lida gasped, "Why? What are you doing?"

"You have a good and noble son, Mrs. Lowenstein. He says he loves you and goodbye." With those words, Thom used his tentacle to pull Prometheus' arm off him. Then he let go.

Prometheus snapped back, flying up and slamming into Buddha. Thom and David plummeted out of the shelter of Buddha's arms, falling toward the Armageddon.

"No!" Lida roared as Thom's consciousness fell back into the memory while his cloud body fell into the belly of Armageddon.

Thom's eternal soul would die, but it was how it had to be. It's what he was born for, he was certain now. Along with David and Abraham, he would stop Armageddon.

Chapter 19
The Unforgiven

Thom stood before the memory of Abraham, the spectral children becoming a grey mist around his waist. He looked into the eyes of the memory of Abraham until he found David.

"I said goodbye to your mom for you."

"But you didn't come back to tell me that," David said, his voice still smothered under a hurricane. "You came to die with me."

Thom smiled. "Three souls exploding, each as bad as Corbin…"

"Worse," David said. "I'm so *angry*, my soul ought to be a block-buster."

"Okay," Thom said, preparing himself to step into the memory of Abraham, preparing to die again—and die for good.

For good.

It really would be for good. His eternal soul would be gone, no after-afterlife, just nothing. And before the nothing, the horrors of Abraham's memory. Horrors seemed minor compared to never seeing Gregory again, never having a chance to make it up to him, to tell him that he'd always loved him, even if Thom was too screwed up to know it the whole time. After all this, Thom could've found Gregory, given him the relationship he deserved. Instead of that, Thom would step into this nightmare and die. This sacrifice would be for Gregory. Thom only hoped Gregory would find joy in an afterlife without Thom in it.

"Okay," Thom said again, "let's kill a god."

Before Thom could enter the memory of Abraham, a booming voice filled the air. "Stop right there! I will not let you hurt my baby boy! And, Abraham, how could you bring your son into this memory?"

Thom staggered back as he gazed up at the vast face of Lida Lowenstein. A hand, one as long as a man is tall, reached out of the sky and scooped the soul of Abraham out of the memory. Before Thom the shadow of Abraham continued to lead the shadow children on their never-ending march. Lida had saved him but not David, not yet. If she did save him, how would they kill Alpha? What would stop Armageddon?

High above Thom, Abraham looked up from the palm of the hand that held him and muttered, "Lida? Is that really you?" He stood and hugged her giant thumb. "Oh, my Lida! I was lost without you. I woke up on a train and...I thought they'd killed you."

"They did kill me," Lida said. "We're both dead. And poor David died too. And then you brought him to this horrible place. Shameful! Now, sort yourself so we can leave."

Abraham said, "I'm dead?"

"You are," said the voice of Peterson.

The memory of the camp and the doomed children dissolved into yellow tinged gas. It swept over Thom, shrouding all. Thom was alone and furious. He balled up his fists, ready to punch

Peterson in the mouth as soon as he could find him. This self-righteous ass needed to be pounded into the ground, and Thom couldn't wait to do the pounding.

But when the mist pulled back, he found himself inside the memory of Lida Lowenstein. Thom, David, Abraham, and the soul of Lida—they all occupied the body of Lida, everyone except Peterson. Still in his SS uniform, Peterson stood apart.

Around them was yellow wallpaper and green living room furniture. It was an apartment. Lida's apartment. At the moment, it was full of Nazis, and she just wasn't having it. She'd been shouting for them to leave her home at once. But the Lieutenant in charge demanded to know where their son was. If *it* was dead like she said, then where were *its* remains, or *its* death papers?

Lida ignored their questions and kept demanding they leave. Her husband intervened, apologizing for his wife. Apologizing for everything. Perhaps they could come back later, when his wife was less upset, and perhaps not as a surprise, if they would be so kind. In reply, the Lieutenant slammed his leather-clad fist into Abraham's jaw, knocking him unconscious. Before her husband's limp body hit the floor, Lida's fist hit the Lieutenant's face. He fell to his ass.

The officer got up. Abraham did not. Lida cocked her fist to hit the Lieutenant again but two of the soldiers grabbed her while a third held a quivering gun in her face. Behind the Luger was a pair of wide eyes, the eyes of a boy who didn't want to be there.

Dramatically drawing a handkerchief to wipe the blood from his mouth, the Nazi officer absently told the frightened child, "Kill her."

The boy didn't kill Lida. He stood shaking, his eyes staring into hers.

"Did you not hear me? Kill her."

The boy in the Nazi uniform, staring into Lida's eyes, still didn't fire. He couldn't. He was not a killer. Lida could see it in him, even in that moment when she knew he would eventually shoot her. He had no choice. He was a victim, just like her.

The Nazi Lieutenant drew his Luger and shoved it under the boy's chin. "Do you not hear me? I said shoot her." He pressed the barrel into the soft flesh. "Fire, now."

Thom stared at that boy through Lida's eyes, terrified and confused. He wanted to save her. He wanted to save himself.

But the memory of Lida smiled at the boy and said, "It's okay."

To the boy's surprise, his gun fired. He jumped as Lida's blood splattered him. His wide, horror-filled eyes remained locked on Lida as she slipped from the hands of the men holding her, and onto the floor. Her blood spread across the living room carpet. Coldness crept into her body. As she faded into death, the poor boy who shot her couldn't stop staring at what he had done. All she wanted to do was hug the boy and assure him that this was not his fault. But she was already gone.

The memory replayed. This time the boy's eyes were angry. Lida did not recognize them and thus Thom did not either. This was the face of the boy who shot her, but not his soul, not even the memory of it. This was something else. The corrupted vision of the boy pulled the trigger with satisfaction. He sneered as he watched Thom and the others, all being Lida, as she crumpled to the floor and bled to death. Then it happened again, the boy's eyes colder and darker this time. Then again with eyes even darker, like demonic pits vanishing into shadow.

Thom's breath came in short huffs, each a gasp before dying, each death more terrifying than the last. Like David's memory of the bullies, they were trapped here, locked in a loop. With each iteration, Thom's horror multiplied. He could feel the same in David and Abraham. Lida was lost in here with them.

He had to do something to get them out of here. He had to stop living this replaying moment, find something else to focus on, something more emotional than being shot to death over and over. Thom turned his focus on Peterson, playing the role of the real killer, the Nazi who'd shoved the gun under the kid's chin, forcing him to commit murder or die. The memory replayed without his help. The twisted version of the boy fired with glee now. Peterson stood back with a disgusting grin smeared across his face. Enraged, Thom focused on Peterson until he pulled his consciousness partly free. It was enough.

"How could you wear that uniform?" Thom demanded, using his anger to muster his will.

But the sound never reached Peterson. Thom's will waned. He was too deep in the memory of Lida. His words couldn't escape; he didn't have the strength. And he was only getting weaker. But maybe someone in this memory with him was stronger. He knew who it had to be. He only hoped he could reach her within her own memory.

"This isn't real," Thom yelled. "Lida! Can you hear me? This isn't what happened."

"Oh," Lida said, her voice distant and muffled by loud wind. "You're David's friend, aren't you?"

This memory must've hit her hard, but at least she was talking. He had to get her to snap out of it. "Yes, it's me Thom. You've got to escape this. We're all in this with you."

"Thom?" she puzzled. "Have we met?"

She was getting worse, not better. Thom's frustration rose, the anger swelling within him. But he wouldn't become a bomb in here because this wasn't like Abraham's memory. Lila's steadfast calm in the face of her own death kept this memory stable. They would not explode. They would not kill a god. They would remain here for an eternity with Peterson overseeing their internment in service to his 'god.' And Thom couldn't stop it. This was Lida's memory; only she could break them free. And only one thing would rouse her.

"Lida!" Thom yelled with all his strength. "David is in trouble!"

"My big brave boy?"

"Yes, David! You need to focus so you can help David! Do you know who I am?"

After a long pause filled with them being shot dead again and again, she said, "Thom?"

"Yes!" he called back.

"David's friend, Thom?"

The gun rose and fired. They died again.

"Yes! I am!" Thom yelled as the memory restarted, his will weakening with each replay. "We have to help David!"

There was another long, death-filled pause, each a gut punch wearing Thom down.

Lida muttered, "Abraham? He was…What happened to that prison camp? Why are we in my living room?"

He had her. "We're trapped in your memory!" Thom yelled to Lida, his strength nearly gone, his mind ready to surrender to this emotional prison. "Me, you, Abraham, and your son, David. We have to get out of this to help David."

"But this isn't what happened," Lida said as the boy raised the gun at them again. To Thom's surprise, she abruptly stepped out of her memory of herself. "That isn't the boy who shot me," she said as she stood next to herself, the self being shot again and again by a boy with demonic eyes. "No, this is not him at all. It just looks like him. But I think I see…"

She reached into the memory of the boy and pulled his consciousness free of it. The young German now stood beside the memory of himself. Instead of his Nazi uniform, he wore a yellowed button-down shirt that had once been white. His pants were dark green wool, held up by frayed suspenders.

Looking at the memory of himself, the young man fell to his knees. "Oh my god," he sobbed into his hands. "I killed her. I killed that woman. How could I?"

Lida put her hand on his shoulder. "It wasn't your fault."

While Thom died again, shot by his doppelganger, the young man looked up at the freed Lida. His face was red and dripping with tears. "It's you. You're that woman." He shivered.

"I'm Lida," she said, casting a warm smile over him. "And you are?"

"I'm…I'm Erwin, and I…I killed you. I am so sorry. Can you ever forgive me?"

She shook her head. "No, I cannot because there's nothing to forgive."

"But I killed you? he questioned.

The memory of the Nazi Lieutenant returned to shoving his gun under the boy's chin. From inside it, Peterson stepped out. His face became his own, but his uniform remained that of the Lieutenant.

Thom tried to step free of the memory of Lida but each time the memory rewound, he found himself still there, his sense of self vanishing little by little.

"Thou shall not murder!" Peterson proclaimed. A dark red glow emanated from him and his Nazi uniform. "Whomever kills another person shall be put to death!"

"I killed you," Erwin sobbed again. "I'm a murderer."

Lida helped the boy to his feet. Looking sternly into his eyes, she said, "You are not a murderer. You did nothing of the sort. That Lieutenant did this to both of us. You pulled that trigger because that Lieutenant forced you to."

"You shall not murder," Peterson bellowed.

Lida pulled Erwin into a hug. "If you hadn't shot me, then that horrible Lieutenant would've done it after he shot you."

Peterson's soul swelled to twenty feet tall, the memory of the apartment growing taller with him. From above, he proclaimed, "Anyone who murders shall be subject to judgement."

Lida waved the back of her hand at Peterson and told Erwin, "Ignore him. He's all bluster. I knew I was going to die the moment I heard your commander banging on my door. I knew they'd come to ask about David, or to just round us up. And I knew it would end like this. But I'm so sorry that you had to pull the trigger."

Still raining tears, Erwin gawked at her. "Why would you apologize to me?"

Lida clasped her hands over her heart. "Because even after the horrible grownups in your life tried so hard to poison you, you still didn't want to kill me. You have a good heart."

Peterson pointed his giant accusing finger down at Lida and Erwin and said, "Whoever believes in Him shall not perish but have eternal life."

While the first copy of Erwin continued to shoot Thom over and over, another twisted copy appeared, one with dark eyes and a dark grin. The new copy aimed at the true Lida and the true Erwin. Then another copy appeared and another, until the copies surrounded Lida and Erwin, all pointing their guns at them, all about to fire. Lida held the boy tighter.

Peterson declared, "I can do all this through Him who gives me strength."

With Peterson distracted, the memory holding Thom weakened. His mind came back into focus. Looking at Peterson in that SS uniform, Thom wanted to rip it off and shove it down his throat. The more he thought about that, the more distant Peterson, Lida, and Erwin seemed. Thom wanted to be angry, but it wasn't helping, it was hurting, driving him back into the memory trap.

Lida's thoughts about Erwin had gotten her out, thoughts of sympathy. Thom needed try something like that. He needed to pull his thought from Peterson in that Nazi getup and focus them on his friends. They needed him. He needed to calm down and help them. He'd led them into this; it was his duty to get them out. With that thought, Thom sensed a crack open in the memory. He stepped through it and into Lida's living room.

The replicated memories of the boy surround him as he stood with Lida and Erwin. The memory of Lida's death continued to play out just behind the circle of evil Erwins.

"Anyone who murders shall be subject to judgement," Peterson declared, looming over them all.

This was truly Peterson. His soul stood before Thom, glowing with dark red emotional light. After all Thom had been through since he died—sharing thoughts, reliving memories, projecting his willpower into David and his dad like a blood transfusion— Thom had tuned his senses to this reality. But he hadn't realized how much until now. He could see past the grim anger emanating from Peterson's soul. He could see into his heart. He could see into Lida's heart and Erwin's heart as well. In them, Thom saw that same light he'd used to keep David from fading into nothing back when they first arrived in this afterlife.

But for Peterson, where that light should've been, Thom sensed only void.

"Who are you to pass judgement?" Thom demanded. "How could you wear that thing and dare to stand judgement over anyone?"

"I speak in the name of the Lord."

Thom scoffed, "Your lord is a lie."

"The Lord is my shepherd, I lack nothing."

"No," Thom said, "You lack something, and I can see it."

"Trust in the Lord with all your heart and lean not on your own understanding."

Thom sneered at him. "Sorry, that's not who I am. I'm a Stoneshield; I was born a strategist and strategy requires the continuous gathering of knowledge. It becomes second nature, constantly analyzing everything around you. It's a habit that I carried into the afterlife. So, I've figured a few things out since I kicked the bucket."

Red smoke gathered around the giant Peterson. "From the tree of the knowledge of good and evil you shall not eat."

"Too late," Thom said. "I already ate, and I learned a lot from that tree. Like these colors I see, they're emotions, but the same color can mean different things. Like the souls of animals that create the ocean, they look gold—to me at least—because they're in bliss. But the gold I see in the cloud of a human soul is happiness, which ain't the same as bliss. And then there's the gold inside me…inside *most* of us."

Peterson grimaced down at Thom. "In much wisdom is much grief: and he that increaseth knowledge, increaseth sorrow."

"That gold inside me ain't happiness or bliss," Thom continued. "I know because I wasn't feeling happy or blissful when I glowed light into David to save him. Afterwards, I kept wondering what it was. I can be a real knucklehead about my own feelings, even when I can see them as colors. On Earth, I had to shut a lot of my feelings off because I was in a world poisoned by people like you. I even shut off my feelings for the man I loved. So, I'm not surprised that I didn't get it at first, but I did get it eventually."

"Every knee shall bow to me," Peterson cried, "and every tongue shall confess to God."

"But you only just now helped me really understand it," Thom said. "I finally get how important that light is because, when I look at your soul, it's not there. You're empty Peterson, a hollow shell of anger."

"For the wrath of God is revealed from heaven against all ungodliness and unrighteousness of men!" Peterson roared.

Thom remained defiantly calm. "My gold is something you lack—*empathy*. It's empathy that has the power to heal another soul. I've taught this to others, but I can't teach you, Peterson. Because in place of empathy, you got nothing. But don't worry. I got empathy to spare. You can have some of mine."

While David and Abraham remained trapped in the memory of Lida, and while the consciousness of Lida cradled the soul of Erwin, Thom opened his arms wide and cast a golden light over the towering Peterson. The ring of Erwins faded from existence but the repeating death of Lida still held Abraham and David.

As the light poured from Thom, the giant Peterson staggered back.

"This is what empathy feels like," he said as he forced the light into Peterson's soul. "Do you have empathy now? Can you see what you've done, how you hurt people? Do you understand now?"

As the empathy filled Peterson, his soul drew Thom into his dark epiphanies. Peterson finally understood what it felt like for Thom or for Lida to look at him in that uniform—the fear, the anger, and the disgust. And torturing them with this memory, what kind of God would ask that of him?

The golden light sank deeper, dredging up memories from Peterson's life, projecting them into Thom. New York, 1943, beating a kid in a zoot suit. He called the kid a traitor for not being in the service, even though Peterson knew the kid wasn't nearly old enough to enlist. It wasn't about patriotism. It wasn't about the zoot suit or even about the kid being Hispanic. It was because he could. It was the Zoot Suit Riots, sanctioned and encouraged by the U.S. Army. Everybody was doing it, and Peterson reveled in it—a chance to beat someone, it didn't matter who or why.

But now he felt it, what it was like to be on the other end of his cruelty. He saw the kid's frightened eyes. He heard the screams of the girlfriend as she watched five American soldiers bludgeon her sixteen-year-old boyfriend in the street, the cops holding people back so the beating could continue.

Then Thom saw Peterson's memory of Corbin. In the name of his Lord, Peterson had refused to let Corbin's soul escape. As it neared critical mass, he knew he should let go, that his Lord would not gain this soul, not then, not that way. Peterson could have and should have let go. But he felt that rush, the same electric high he felt during the riots. So, he held on until Corbin's soul exploded.

"I did these things?" the giant Peterson muttered.

He fell to his knees. His massive presence grew larger, filling the small apartment, stretching it higher and wider as he grew.

"The pain I caused…" Peterson dropped his face in his hands. "How could I?"

He hunched into heavy sobs, his soul growing darker and darker. Black lightning fired from him, destroying the ceiling and walls. In their place, a tornado of black and grey clouds whipped around them. Thom stood on the remains of the apartment floor, with Lida and Erwin huddled beside him, and David and Abraham still locked in Lida's replaying memory.

Over the thunder and wind, Thom called to Lida, "He's becoming an emotional bomb. He's going to explode. We need to get everyone out of here! But David and Abraham…?"

Still holding Erwin, Lida said, "We can save them. We just need a little help." To Erwin she said, "I need you bring your mother here. Just call to her. Tell her you need help."

Almost immediately, the soul of Erwin's mother appeared beside him. The German boy embraced her.

"Wow," Thom gasped. "But how?"

Lida said, "She's his mom. Of course, she came. And here come the others."

"The others?"

"Yes, the others who heard Erwin," Lida said. "Didn't you feel it, all their souls waking up just now? I did. Look, here they come."

Lida pointed into the darkness of the spinning smog. A soft, golden light rose in the distance. It drew closer until it came into focus. The gathering light became hundreds of women from around the world and throughout time, all in their Earthly garments, all glowing gold. But these were not the moms of Lida's choir. These women had been trapped in Alpha, but awakened by Erwin, then called together by Lida. With the monster weakened, they were able to free themselves from their soul well-induced nightmares and gather to help a child.

They stood together within the swirling darkness as if on solid ground. A handful of them walked forward into the remains of the apartment. They surrounded the memory of Lida's death and glowed empathy into it. The Lieutenant, the memory of Lida, and the dark version of Erwin all disappeared. David and Abraham were free but dazed.

The giant Peterson began to shrink, becoming smaller and brighter, his sobs melting into a defining moan.

Thom told Lida, "We got to go now, like right now. Can your choir pull us out?"

"No need to pull," Lida said, entirely too calmly for Thom's liking. "We can open the door."

Peterson was getting small and brighter. They didn't have time to meditate like Buddha had, if that's what she planned. They probably didn't have time to pull everyone out either. But whatever they did, they had to do it now if they were going to save anyone at all.

Thom snapped at Lida, "What door? How? There's no time!"

"Oh, it'll take no time," Lida promised. "And it'll be easier for these ladies since I've done it before with the other ladies, the ones in my choir. Since there's so many of us here, it should be as easy as when my choir left that dark place."

Lida turned her attention to the moms and conveyed a thought to them. Thom felt it go by like a breeze, but he didn't catch it for himself. Then Lida and her many moms closed their eyes and hummed. A bright golden glow emanated from them, pushing back the swirling shadows. All as one, they looked up. A crack opened in the spinning black above, revealing the golden ocean of the animalsphere beyond.

"We must hurry, ladies," Lida said. "Gather the children."

Around the women appeared new specters, small ones, each just a child. Mothers and children joined hands and lifted off, surging upward through the breach. As the last of them ascended, Lida took the hands of the still befuddled Abraham and David and followed the others.

Peterson's soul continued to shrink, growing brighter and brighter as it did. The dark clouds spun around him.

Someone took Thom's hand and carried him up behind all the others. It was Erwin's mother lifting him and the boy to safety. They were last to reach the breach. Before they entered, Thom looked back. Lida's living room was gone. All that remained was black clouds whipping around Peterson's shrinking bright ball of a soul. Thom had done it. The empathy he gave Peterson had started something that couldn't be stopped. Alpha was going to die, Thom was certain.

Erwin's mom pulled Thom's soul into the breach. Passing through, Thom became a cloud again, a ball of thick red smoke swimming up through the golden ocean. Behind him, he saw Alpha, now the Armageddon of Earth. The massive black sphere spread wider than all of New York City. Gazing upon it, Thom felt cold.

The breach was still open with Peterson inside it, glowing like a tiny sun. But he was dwarfed by what Alpha had become. What if that thing survived Peterson's death? Even crippled, it could recover and become unstoppable. Thom needed to make sure that thing died here and now. He had to get back in there and explode with Peterson. It was the only way to be sure.

Thom turned and frantically swam back down. But it was too late.

Peterson exploded.

A wall of bright white raced up at Thom. When it struck, his consciousness experienced a billion deaths at once, each different but all happening at the same time. Thom was murdered, committed suicide, died naturally, and died stupidly. He felt cold water filling his lungs, salty and fresh, oily and clean. He felt the blood drain from his body, his lungs collapse, his heart stop, his throat swell shut. He saw the mob coming for him, a bus, a car, a train, a wall of fire. He was mauled by bears, wolves, and panthers. Each death was horrible, and they all happened to him at the same time.

Then there was nothing.

Chapter 20
A New Afterlife

"Are you okay?"

As the afterlife came into focus, Thom found his soul to be spread wide into a red mist upon the golden ocean. Above him hovered two silver spheres, one almost twice the size of the other. They glowed empathy into Thom.

"Are you okay?" asked the larger one again. "Buddha had us take care of you while you recovered."

It was the Erwin's mother. Her son's soul was the smaller orb standing beside her.

"Yeah," Thom said. With some effort, he pulled himself back into a red orb. "I'm okay. Just dazed."

They stopped feeding him energy.

All around Thom, souls bubbled to the surface while choirs descended to greet and help them. Even the choirs of Confucius and Nietzsche had returned to help the survivors. But Lida's choir of moms had dissolved into individuals, spreading themselves far and wide, shining gold into the newly arriving souls to keep them from fading.

Thom saw a trio of two solid sliver orbs and one green one. While the green sphere of Abraham merely followed, the silver orbs of Lida and David moved across the surface helping the newly freed. For the moment, Lida had shrunk herself to merely twice the size of David.

"Thank you so much for helping my son," Erwin's mother said to Thom. "And for saving me too. I don't know how to thank you."

"I think the person we need to thank is over there." Thom gestured toward Lida.

Without interrupting her work, Lida said, "You're wrong, Thom. If you hadn't stopped that Lieutenant, I'd still be punching him. We'd never have gotten out."

"She's right," said Thom's dad, coming up behind him. Like Lida and David, his soul had become a silver orb. "I've been sharing memories with the Lowensteins. Everyone had a role, but you're the hero. I couldn't be prouder, Thom."

"Thank you, Dad." Thom looked at himself, a solid orb of red. His dad had found the nirvana thing. Why hadn't Thom?

His dad said, "No, thank you, Thom. You saved the love of my life."

Another orb of solid silver emerged from behind his father.

"Mom? Since you left the church…I thought you'd have…"

"Faded? That makes sense. But no, I've been in…" She trailed off, her orb dimming momentarily. "I'd rather not talk about it."

"I'm so sorry, Mom. If I'd known—"

"I know. And don't worry about it. I'm here now," she said, inching closer. "We are both so proud of you, Thom."

Thom's inner gold glowed bright, beaming through his solid red shell, inadvertently adding strength to weak souls gathered in puddles around him, helping them ascended toward the choirs above.

As Snake and Prometheus approached, Snake said, "Wow, look at the glow on you, Thom."

Thom's dad said, "We can have a family reunion later. Right now, we should help the others. There's a lot of wounded. Beatrice, can you do Thom's glowing thing?"

Thom's mom said, "Don't know. Let's see."

As Thom and the others watched, she hovered near a puddle. For a moment, nothing happened. Thom was about to demonstrate when a faint glow rose. It slowly brightened, shining upon the puddle. The soul soon had enough strength to become a cloud. It rose away to join the choir of Nietzsche.

Beatrice said, "That was good. I could've done better; I mean...*Nietzsche*. So pessimistic."

"God is dead. God remains dead. And we have killed him," Nietzsche bellowed.

"That was plenty good," his dad said, ignoring Nietzsche. "We'd better start helping."

Prometheus said, "Thom, before you join the others. I wanted to show you something."

"We're hoping you can do something that we couldn't," Snake said.

While his mom and dad joined the many others tending to the waning souls, Thom followed Prometheus and Snake to two puddles that had pooled side by side. They were both the same murky green. It was a deep dark sickening green the like Thom had never seen.

"What are they?" he asked.

Prometheus said, "That's Alpha and Unum."

Snake said, "Or you could say Suum and Boko…or 'hair' and 'arm.' In his life, they called Unum 'arm' because he had big arms and they called Alpha 'hair' because he had big hair. Names were simpler back then."

"They are two of the oldest human souls in existence," Prometheus said. "And they are fading. Despite all they did, we tried to save them."

"We really did," Snake swore.

"Our efforts did little. We were hoping you could help."

"We don't think they're dangerous anymore," Snake explained. "No one's ever going to join a choir of them again. So, saving them seems the decent thing to do."

Thom turned to Prometheus, "Even after Alpha betrayed you, you want to save him?"

"No, but it's the right thing to do."

Snake said, "And if they try to become soul wells again, we know how to take them apart. Do you think you can do anything for them?"

Thom said. "I don't know, but I'll try."

Thom hovered between the two puddles shining golden light upon both souls at once. He glowed as bright as he could, but the light seemed to do nothing, like it couldn't penetrate their darkness. With both of them fading before his eyes, Thom instinctively reached out to help. When he touched the puddles, Thom found himself in two memories at once.

He was a teen, sitting by the mouth of a cave, guarding the entrance while the others slept. The floor of the cave spilled out into the forest like a grey stone tongue. Shattered black rocks lay scattered across it. A frigid wind whipped through the dark dry forest, rustling dead leaves. Thom pulled his animal skins tighter around himself and shivered.

In the other memory, Thom was also a teen, but running across a grassy plain in daylight, his feet bare but rugged, his body wrapped in tanned hides. In his hands, a long, roughly carved stone-tipped spear. Cresting the low rise in the land, he saw the two horns first, black curving bone as wide as seven men from point to point. The mighty goring weapons sat atop a beast as tall as two men and as strong as a hundred. It was an aurochs, and his tribe had never killed one before.

In the cave memory, someone whispered in Thom's ear. He turned, looking for who it was , but his tribe all slept. Thom was almost certain he'd heard Prometheus' voice telling him to bang the black rocks together, but memory Thom wasn't sure if he'd heard anything at all. Spooked, memory Thom backed against the wall. Nothing moved. No other sounds came. He gradually relaxed. In the moonlight before him, the black rocks stood out against the grey. As if compelled by some spell, he picked up two of them and banged them together; they made a spark. It amused him. As the night dragged on, he kept making sparks, a delightful distraction from his dull duty. One of the sparks landed on his long scraggly hair, setting it on fire. Thom danced around, grunting, and swatting it out.

In the aurochs memory, Thom ran down a slope, ripping a path through tall grass. His brothers and cousins had done as he instructed. And it worked! They isolated the bull while the rest of the herd stampeded away. From every side, they stabbed at it with the longer spears that Thom had instructed them to make. The bull reared and thrashed, but Thom's kin kept the beast contained. Racing down the hill toward the chaos, he readied his own spear. The other hunters just needed to keep the beast there a moment longer.

In the cave memory, his hair continued to smolder and flame; only the built-up oil and sweat kept it from lighting his whole head on fire. He pounded on it with his palms to no avail. Finding a sharp stone, he cut off the smoldering ends and threw them out into the surrounding brush. They landed on a small, dry bush growing from a crevice in the stone ground. The bush caught fire. Thom approached the flame. It was warm. He put more dried bushes on it. He got warmer.

In the other memory, the aurochs swung its horns into Thom's younger brother, impaling his gut. The beast reared back, lifting his brother high. He was still alive, but not really. Thom was not bothered by the loss. Death was too common to be distracted by it. And Thom needed to focus. If this worked, his tribe would have more meat than they'd ever imagined.

Shutting out his brother's screams, Thom charged at the aurochs and drove his stone-tipped spear into the monster's throat. The beast screeched and gurgled. Thom pushed the spear in deeper. The animal staggered sideways, taking Thom's weapon with it. Then the beast collapsed dead. The hunters cheered.

After the kill, they call him Boko, their word for arm. From that day on, Boko became the leader of the hunts. In his late twenties, an aurochs gored him to death like his brother. In the afterlife, he continued to organize others. Despite Snake and Prometheus trying to prevent it, Boko became Earth's first soul well, Unum.

In the cave memory, Thom had the warmest night of winter guard duty ever. The next day he showed the rest of his tribe what he'd done with the rocks, again using his hair as kindling, something the others immediately saw as unnecessary. They realized that dead leaves work and smell better than burning hair.

But still, Thom had changed the lives of his tribe, thanks to a whisper from Prometheus. Afterwards, they called him Suum, their word for hair. In the afterlife, he becomes a friend to Prometheus. Together they fight Unum, until Suum becomes Alpha.

***

"You okay, Thom?" Snake asked.

Shaking off the memories, Thom looked around the animal-sphere; the dim puddles were gone. "Where are Boko and Suum...or whatever you want to call them?"

Prometheus said, "They faded from existence while you were attached to them."

"We thought you might fade too," Snake said. "We're glad you didn't."

"They're gone?" Thom looked around the surface again. There was no trace of them but there were many other souls still bubbling up from below, and there were many souls and choirs waiting to help the newly freed.

Snake said, "Yup, gone. No soul wells, no Armageddon, just gone."

Connected to them as they faded, their whole lives and after-lives played out before Thom's eyes, their experiences flashing before him. Now all that remained of them was his memories of their memories.

Thom took a breath. He couldn't save those two souls. But Thom and everyone else had saved the world from them. Somehow, instead of feeling relieved or triumphant, he felt lost, liked he'd completed his mission...all his missions, with nothing left to do. The war was over, and he didn't die this time. He asked, "So, now what?"

Prometheus said, "You defeated your Armageddon. No one has ever done that before. So, I have no idea."

"*Well*, I have an idea," Snake said, turning his attention to Prometheus.

"Really?" Prometheus asked, exasperated.

"Please. I mean, we killed an Armageddon; if that's not the time, come on?"

"Okay, fine."

"Really, I can?"

"Before I change my mind."

Snake's silver orb grew two silver tentacles. He used them to hug Prometheus. Though Thom perceived Prometheus releasing a heavy sigh, Prometheus' silver orb also grew tentacles and hugged Snake back.

"Are you happy now?" Prometheus asked.

"I am."

Prometheus said, "Then so am I." They continued to hug.

"Thom?" said a pair of voices in unison.

He turned to see the familiar dyad of Sara and Andrea. They were still a single orb, but they'd become solid and silver like so many others around him. It seemed like everyone else who'd fought in the battle had changed, but Thom remained a red orb. What was wrong with him?

Still in unison, Andrea and Sara said, "We have someone who wants to see you."

Andrea and Sara moved aside. Thom saw another orb of silver. This soul was new, but Thom immediately recognized it. He drifted toward it as it drifted toward him. A few feet apart, they stopped.

"Hi, Thom. I've missed you."

"Gregory? You...here..." Thom felt like his knees had buckled; his cloud-self sank to the surface. "You were in Alpha but now..."

"I was somewhere," Gregory said. "It was dark, and it kept showing me things that I knew weren't true, trying to use you as a weapon. It wasn't working but I couldn't get out."

"I'm so sorry," Thom said, as he pulled himself up. "When we were alive, I...I didn't know...all that time...all that wasted time..." His red shell darkened.

"It's okay," Gregory said.

"No," Thom said, "it's not. I wasted your life because I was too afraid to be who I really was. I should've known better."

287

Gregory floated closer. "How could you've known better? You didn't even know who you were." Gregory created a silver arm and reached out for Thom. "But we're here now. We have another chance."

Growing even darker, Thom said, "I just wish we could do it all again...do it right."

"You mean like this?" With his silver arm, Gregory touched Thom, pulling him into a memory.

Thom was Thom. He wore jeans and a T-shirt that reeked of dirt and sweat. He sat on a log, looking out across a wooded valley. A couple miles away, halfway up the gradual slope on the far side, a herd of deer grazed. That would be their day, catching up with the herd, taking down a buck. But for the moment, coffee. As Thom sat looking at the beautiful mist-shrouded valley, Gregory walked up behind him with two tin cups of bitter coffee. He sat and handed one to Thom.

Unlike in the original memory, Gregory sat close, his arm around Thom's waist. Thom in turn rested his head of Gregory's shoulder. Then the memory transformed into another. They went from a hunting trip to a fishing trip. They sat together in a wooden canoe, only instead of being at opposite ends, they lay together in the middle. Thom relaxed in Gregory's strong arms. The dream changed again. Thom was still in Gregory's arms but this time they were in a tent. It was cold and they were sharing a sleeping bag.

Looking into Gregory's tranquil blue eyes, Thom couldn't imagine how he'd managed to not know that he was in love with him. So much precious time wasted. And why? But Thom had him here and now. He inched forward. Their lips drew closer.

"Wait, not yet," Gregory said. "You made me a promise."

The memory changed once more, but not into a memory that belonged to either of them. Gregory had gotten this one from another soul. In this borrowed memory, Thom wore his D-Day uniform, clean and no gear. Gregory wore his uniform as well, also clean and unencumbered. Around them was a stadium, one they'd both seen in newsreels. It was Zeppelin Field, a part of the Nazi parade grounds.

Thom said, "This isn't Berlin. We promised to meet in Berlin."

"No," Gregory said, "it's Nierenberg. And it's better. Watch."

Gregory tossed his head to the side and Thom glanced over to see a giant swastika within a ring of leaves overlooking the parade grounds, a part of Hitler's massive pulpit. Seeing it filled Thom with disgust. He wanted to rip it down with his bare hands. From somewhere beyond his sight, a tank fired. It filled the air with smoke and noise. The Nazi symbol shattered into stone and dust. A great plume of smoke rose into the sky.

"And that really happened," Gregory said. "That's how the war ended."

Thom turned to Gregory and said, "You're right, this is better."

Then they kissed. It wasn't a memory. It was a real, it was now, and it was far overdue. Though they were still inside this memory, Thom could feel his cloud body transform into a silver sphere.

He still didn't understand what nirvana was, but he knew what it felt like. It felt like Gregory in his arms.

***

It was a new day in a new afterlife. In the east, the sun had only just begun to rise; not really a sun, but a choir, the last and only remaining true choir of old, the one that had been the bright silver choir majestic of Buddha. Having achieved collective nirvana, the Choir of Buddha no longer required his constant guidance. Thus, Buddha himself was no longer a part of it, but it glowed brighter than it ever had before, and it glowed for all of Earth's afterlife, regularly orbiting the animalsphere, finally creating a division of night and day.

But Thom woke in a memory of daytime. He jumped out of bed and was instantly dressed for playing in the woods with his friends, though that was not what he had planned. Nor did he have a date with Gregory this time. Today was special.

He entered the living room of his second-floor apartment to find his mom sipping coffee, listening to the radio, and smoking a cigar. "Good morning, Sleepyhead," she said. "Your father already left. He said he'd meet you there."

"Thanks, Mom," Thom said as he hugged her. "What're you going to do today?"

Lifting her cigar, she said, "I'm already doing it."

He chuckled, kissed her goodbye, and then opened the door to what should've been the stairs down to the street. Instead, it opened to a city of tall, narrow structures. Thom stepped through the door of his apartment, onto the golden ocean, and into his adult body and military dress uniform. Behind him the door closed and vanished. Where it had been, there stood a tall spike of silver light, narrower than the now-absent door.

After so many souls had escaped the wells and reunited with lost loved ones, Earth's afterlife experienced a widespread Nirvana, a term Thom now understood to be a calm balance within oneself, or the feeling of Gregory in his arms.

The afterlife was safe and peaceful but also brimming with bright silver choirs. The overcrowded sky soon merged and sank to the surface, reforming into glimmering spires of silver that made better use of the abundant vertical space. These towers gradually migrated across the golden ocean and clustered together, becoming cities scattered across the afterlife.

Like the choirs they evolved from, each spire was made of the many souls within it. And each acted as a gateway to another time and place, like Thom's spire of twentieth century North America. Across from it was the spire of nineteenth century North America, and a spire of the American Colonial era. Around them stood other spires made of souls joined by time, place, experience, or philosophy. They had replaced the cloud choirs, all but the one choir now rising in the east.

Around Thom, other souls in their various earthly forms roamed the streets of the city of spires. Others chose to be spheres drifting through its sky. All were as solid as when they were alive, but even those in their human bodies glowed with an aura of silver. Today, Thom's silver body glowed brighter than usual in anticipation of a special event.

He meandered through the streets, greeting those he passed, making his way to the city's edge. In the open fields beyond, animal souls sprang in and out of individual existence as the mood fit them. Human souls also walked amongst the herds, packs, prides, and flocks. The people here searched the fields for new souls rising from Earth in need of guidance, especially those who'd stayed below long after death. David had been leading expeditions to the Earth to rescue the lost souls. He'd been quite successful. Few ghosts remained. Even Sergeant First Class Williamson had come to join them in the afterlife.

Though Thom had somewhere to be, he paused to greet a friend. "How are you today, Buddha?"

Buddha nodded and smiled, then returned to his task. He knelt, his orange and green robes spilling over him. He reached a hand down, turning the golden ocean to silver wherever he touched it. A little girl stood beside him, her soul appearing as her ten-year-old self in a yellow sun dress. While she watched, Buddha closed his eyes and glowed silver deep into the animalsphere. The fog in front of him swirled about until it coalesced. It leapt out of the ocean and into the girl's arms in the form of a cat.

"Princess!" the little girl cried as she hugged her pet from life. "Thank you, Mr. Buddha!"

Buddha smiled, and the girl ran off. He then bent down again, this time drawing a deer from the ocean. It became a ghostly silver version of its earthly self, then sprang off toward a herd of other deer running between the cities.

"Hello, Thom," Buddha said. "Have you seen Prometheus and Snake today?"

"No, I haven't. Something happen? Did Prometheus go back to being a ball?"

Like almost everyone else in the afterlife, Snake had taken to staying in his living form, a snake-like being with a diamond head and twelve small tentacles in pairs down length of his body. After a little prodding, Prometheus had also returned to his former form, with its humanish torso, three fingers with a thumb-talon, and legs with backwards knees. He had tall black eyes, two long flap-covered nostril slits, and brown down where hair should've been. From his back sprouted two broad angelic wings of white feathers with brown splotches.

Buddha said, "No, Prometheus is still himself, at least he was an hour ago when I saw him. He and Snake were working on their beacon. They've made notable progress."

Prometheus and Snake had been trying to create a transmitter of a sort, something that could project emotional light in controlled intervals. They formed it out of some of the passive souls within the animalsphere. If it worked, and if they could get a response from another world, they planned to project memories…or at least try to. If they did, they'd be able to tell other worlds how to save themselves.

"So, it's almost done?"

"Yes, and it's a sight to behold. They expect to be able to transmit any day now. Soon, the whole universe will know how to stop an Armageddon."

Thom looked up, imagining what Earth must look like to the afterlives of other worlds, a bright silver light in the darkness, he imagined. He looked forward to seeing another silver light in the sky.

"I'll have to drop by and see how it looks later," Thom said. He gazed toward the glowing disk of silver rising over the horizon and added, "Nice sunrise today. Thank you for that."

"You should thank them, not me. Have you been up there to visit?"

"No but I hear it's really nice. They recreated Shangri-La?"

Buddha nodded. "You should take Gregory. I think the two of you would enjoy it."

"I'll do that. But not today."

"You have your banquet today," Buddha said. "Did Lida help with it?"

"Help?" Thom chuckled. "She took over. I can't wait to see what she's done."

"Well, then you better get there. I'm sure the others are waiting. Give my best to Lida."

"I certainly will." Thom strode on, waving goodbye.

Thom walked to one of the spires on the outskirts of the neighboring city. He walked into its silver light and found himself walking up a grassy hillside, still in his D-Day uniform, clean and pressed. Upon the hill's crest stood a mead hall built of roughly hewn timbers. Thom's father waited by the door.

"You look good in your uniform," Thom's dad called to him.

"So do you." Thom looked over his dad's dress uniform from the First Great War. "I think this is the first time I've seen you with all your medals."

"It is. I never got to wear any of these before I died. And that one was awarded posthumously, or so I've been told."

"I have one of those, too." Thom tapped the purple heart on his chest. "You know, they're not handing out war medals like they used to down there."

His dad chuckled. "That tends to happen when peace breaks out."

Thom tossed his head toward the mead hall. "Is everyone in there?"

A broad grin spread over his dad's face. "Let's get inside. I have a surprise for you."

When they entered the mead hall, Thom expected to see a long table with seven chairs. After all, this was a banquet for the line of Stoneshields, but only the ones bearing the name of the American patriot and Founding Father, Thomas Jefferson. Thus Thom, being the seventh and last of that namesake, was surprised to see an eighth chair and six men already sitting at the table.

One of them stood. He wore a uniform from after Thom's time. Thom turned to his dad.

His dad said, "Son, I want to introduce you to Thomas Jefferson Stoneshield VIII."

"What? How?"

"My dad's brother, your Great Uncle Marv, he had a grandson who found out who you were and what you did on D-Day."

"My father named me after you," said Stoneshield the Eighth. "You were his hero. Mine too. When I was ten, we went to Normandy to visit your grave."

Thom muttered, "I'm...I'm honored."

"The honor is mine," the Eighth said.

Thom's dad said, "And there's a Ninth and a Tenth now too."

"My kid and his kid," the Eighth said. "They're still alive but I know they'll be delighted to meet you after they die."

Thom shook his hand. "And I'll be delighted to meet them. I hope it's not until they're good and old."

Thom's dad gesturing toward the table. "I think it's time to eat."

Upon the heavy wooden table, food appeared. There were chicken legs, turkey legs, legs of lamb, as well as two whole geese and one whole wild boar. This was a table set for warriors to tell war stories while they devoured meat.

As Thom took his seat at the head of the table, he realized that Prometheus had been wrong about something. He'd told Thom that he was not seeing or hearing, he was perceiving and receiving. All he experienced was filtered through his own interpretation, filtered through the senses he remembered from life. Prometheus had said that in time that would change, the filters would vanish and so would his senses. He'd lose his sight and hearing, replaced by something new, something that Thom never understood and never would, because Prometheus was wrong.

Not only had he continue to see and hear, but Thom had also regained another of his earthly senses. Looking across the feast before him, Thom realized that everything smelled delicious.

***

And that's what happened.

Bringing these words to you has cost the poor fellow writing this his friends, loved ones, and physical and mental health. Even as he writes these final words, he still believes this to be fiction and that this story is one of his own mind. He has forsaken his own wellbeing to write this, going without food or sleep—something that had never been my intent. I guess that's what hearing a disembodied voice in your head will do to you. I regret the cost, but I felt it necessary to bring this story to you, if for no other reason than to prevent the rise of another soul well.

I still visit the living, and not just to torture this poor guy with my voice in his head. When I do visit, I see the continuing rise of disbelief in humanity, coupled with an eye toward the stars. If we ever reach another civilization, either as souls or as living beings, I hope these words can help them save their afterlife the way that we saved ours.

Scott Coon is an award-winning short story writer, author of the sci-fi novel *LOST HELIX*, and a former U.S. Army Intelligence Analyst. For his service in Kuwait, he received a Central Command Combat Patch and the Joint Service Achievement Award from the NSA. His short stories can be found in *Dark Horses: The Magazine of Weird Fiction*, *MOBIUS: The Journal for Social Change*, *Bewildering Stories*, the anthology *ALIEN GAZE*, and others. Scott Coon shares his knowledge of writing through his YouTube channel and website, as well as in The STEAM Journal at Claremont University.